Union Transfer
Thursday July 26, 2018
Doors: 7:30 | Show: 8:30
Ticket 756 General Admission 158058503 ADVANCED
The Hold Steady
Brooklyn Bowl
61 Wythe Avenue Brooklyn, NY
Fri Dec 1, 2017 9:00 PM
Price:$40.00
21 and over
MW00656890
Order:094171794068 Purchased By:Eric Sweitzer
SECTION GA
ROW GA
SEAT GA
NO REFUNDS/EXCHANGES
Presents
The Hold Steady
Doors open at 7:00PM
THU AUG 14, 2008
NO REFUNDS/EXCHANGES
Opening Act: Purling Hiss
Doors Open at 6:30 pm
Musikfest Cafe presented by Yuengling
ArtsQuest Center 101 Founders Way
Row/Table Seat
Individual $ 22.00
per person food and beverage minimum on all table/bar seating
Purchased By:Britton Mundy
GEN'L ADMISSION 16.00
EAST COAST INDEPENDENT
THE HOLD STEADY
WITH SPECIAL GUESTS
ELEANOR RIGBY'S
603 RTE 6 JERMYN,PA 18433
FRI APR 9 2010 7:00PM
29MAR10
THE GROG SHOP PRESENTS
THE HOLD STEADY
TIM BARRY
$2 DOOR IF UNDER 21
BEACHLAND BALLROOM
15711 Waterloo Road, Cleveland, OH
02/01/14 9:00P DRS@8:00
PRICE:20.00 FEES:6.02 ORDER:MR984QH83
ticketfly
The Horseshoe Tavern's 67th Birthday Celebration
The Hold Steady
The Horseshoe Tavern
370 Queen Street West Toronto, ON
Sat Dec 13, 2014 - Doors: 9:00 PM
Price:$25.50
19 and over; www.horseshoetavern.com
Order:097528726444 Purchased By:Britton Mundy
www.ticketfusion.com/all3
Sun Aug 10th, 2008 9:00 pm
All3 Entertainment Presents:
THE HOLD STEADY
w/ THE LOVED ONES
THE POUR HOUSE
1977 Maybank Highway
Charleston, SC 29412
Doors open at 8:00pm
07/09/2008 8974116 4119379
THE BOWERY PRESENTS
18 & OVER W/ ID
2018 8PM DOORS
Asbury Park, NJ
Admission
+ $1 RESTORE FEE 18.50
Y-ROCK & XPN WELCOME
THE HOLD STEADY
WWW.THETROC.COM
TROCADERO THEATRE
10TH & ARCH STS., PHILA
TUE OCT 05 2010 DRS 7PM
21JUN10
ticketmaster
Artist Presale
ORDER NUMBER 2410812
8619202
ticketfly

THE GOSPEL OF THE HOLD STEADY

HOW A RESURRECTION REALLY FEELS

BY MICHAEL HANN
& THE HOLD STEADY

AKASHIC BOOKS
BROOKLYN, NEW YORK

Published by Akashic Books

ISBN: 978-1-63614-095-7
Library of Congress Control Number: 2022947068

First printing

Cover design by Sohrab Habibion and Nick Holloman
Interior design and layout by Sohrab Habibion

Printed in China

Akashic Books
Brooklyn, New York
Instagram, Twitter, Facebook: AkashicBooks
info@akashicbooks.com
www.akashicbooks.com

TABLE OF CONTENTS

INTRODUCTION

I'M IN THE AMERICAN AIRLINES lounge at LAX tonight after flying from Australia. We left Melbourne last night, a Tuesday. Supposedly it's 11:03 p.m. here, also Tuesday night, but it feels like no time at all. In thirty minutes I'll board another flight to Chicago to connect to another flight to Nashville where we'll play a show, followed by an early morning flight to Atlanta for a show there.

Back in 2014 I was at a festival in the UK and making small talk with the bass player of the Kaiser Chiefs. I was speaking of another grueling flight the next morning (Gatwick to Tampa with a show *the same day*) and he gave me sage advice: if you ever find yourself hurrying through an airport, remember it's because you're lucky enough to have someone on the other side who really wants you there. I've gotten a lot of advice over the last twenty years, but this might be the best. We are only embarking on these laborious trips because it will make a bunch of people happy on the other side.

Especially us, of course. I'm confident that Friday in Nashville and Saturday in Atlanta will be filled with friendly faces who sing along and raise their beers. I'm also confident that when we hit the stage and launch into the opening number, I will feel a rush of elation that I don't get anywhere else. I will look around at my fellow band members during a song and feel grateful and proud to be onstage with them. I will feel joyful. We will play and sing and dance and shout and high-five after the show. If it's a particularly good night, we will look into the crowd and see two people who didn't know each other before the show grab each other and scream lyrics into each other's faces.

As we make our way around the world on these flights, it's good to know what awaits. (I'm now in the American Airlines lounge at O'Hare. It's 7:05 a.m. according to my computer; I'm dubious.)

We are not household names, but our small flame burns extremely hot. When we first started touring, we talked about building a community, to have people who supported the band be able to feel a part of it. Other bands have done it—the Clash is the one that seemed most legendary to us, and I myself felt it in the late-'80s hardcore scene. Somehow our loose beer-soaked plans on this front have coalesced into a hard truth. Our fan base is as committed and dedicated as any fan base in rock and roll. They fly all over the world to see us. They sing every word. They debate among themselves and sometimes with us if they find us in the bar after the show. The number of THS-inspired tattoos rivals any band of our size, especially outside of metal and hardcore. I see them along the arms when they raise up in the crowd, punctuating a specific lyric or just punching the air.

The fans feel a part of it because they *are* a part of it, probably the biggest part of it. These days when I talk to someone who is going to see The Hold Steady for the first time, I already know what they're going to say afterward: "I couldn't stop watching the crowd." Yeah, I know. I've been watching them for twenty years and I still find it miraculous and life-affirming. Ours is a dance that requires a partner. We couldn't have even done it without you . . .

Two decades into this band, the origins of it still feel laughably unambitious. In the absolute beginning, we had serious debates on whether we were going to ever play a show or record. From Tad and my days in Lifter Puller, we'd (perhaps correctly) surmised that a lot of trouble starts when you start moving amps around. It was suggested that we could distill the best part of our version of rock and roll in a single set place, in this case our practice room. And while we did finally break our pledge and set out to play a great many shows in a great many places far and wide in the past two decades, it might be noted that the residency model we've come up with in recent years echoes some part of the original feeling—epic load-ins and load-outs are not what makes a band epic.

To me, the most thrilling development of the last five years of The Hold Steady is the new music we've created. The mood is consistently upbeat and we've been able to channel the good vibes into new songs that are incredibly exciting to us, which makes the shows even more fun. I believe that is an important development that fuels the present version of the band. As for the future? When a band turns twenty, it's hard to have a crystal-clear view of what's next beyond continuing to make music and play shows. But that's been the only real plan for quite a while, and it's gotten us here—traveling far and wide to play music for people who care a lot, doing it on our terms, with friendships intact. We are not the biggest band in the world, but that seems incredibly successful to me. (By the way, we made it to Nashville, though I've stopped looking at clocks.)

I am fifty years old, I've been in this band for almost twenty of them. The Hold Steady didn't change my life, it *is* my life. And if you've read this far, it's likely yours too. Our songs are mainly fiction, but they try to be very honest at the same time. So at the end of each show we say and scream and shout all together a benediction: "We Are All The Hold Steady!" That way, each night we leave the stage with a truth.

Thanks for listening. Thanks for understanding.

Stay Positive,
Craig Finn

35

35

35

35

35

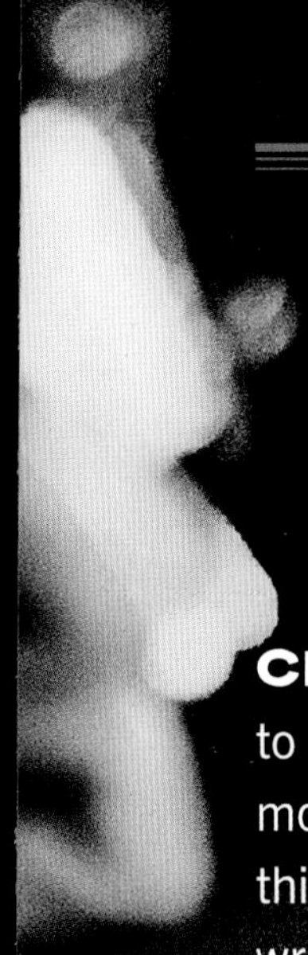

ONE

PARTIES WITH GUITARS

CRAIG FINN (SINGER, GUITARIST, THE HOLD STEADY): After Lifter Puller broke up, I moved to New York. I thought I was done with music, certainly done with touring. Lifter Puller was kinda moving uphill a lot of the time. We didn't have an agent; we didn't have a big record label. Everything was such a struggle. I didn't want to be a part of that kind of touring, but I thought I'd still write songs, and I did. I was even trying to work on some studio stuff. My friend Matt Henderson and I were recording songs in a studio he owned, one of which was "Certain Songs," the original version of that. And one was a song that contained some of the lyrics for "Charlemagne in Sweatpants." But we were thinking of a Steely Dan–esque studio project that doesn't play live.

GALEN POLIVKA (BASSIST, THE HOLD STEADY): My old band had played with Lifter Puller in Minneapolis on several occasions, and then Craig moved to New York. I don't know if I cornered him at the Mercury Lounge, but I'd heard that Lifter Puller broke up and I said, "Not to be morbid or anything, but if you want to start something musically, I'm in, and I'd love to play bass for you." He basically told me to calm down: "I moved here ten days ago, I'm still sorting some stuff out."

CRAIG FINN: I knew he was a great bass player. I wasn't ready to start something but I made a mental note. He was always someone who I admired the way he played, and knew he had the right temperament.

JUDD COUNSELL (DRUMMER, THE HOLD STEADY): Galen and I were in a band called Punchdrunk. We moved to New York in the mid-'90s and tried to make a go of it and couldn't make it work.

GALEN POLIVKA: Craig actually described us as Wire if Wire was a country band. That's far more interesting-sounding than we actually were.

JUDD COUNSELL: At the tail end of that, Craig was talking to us about moving to New York City and wanted to get a sense of how it was going. Lifter Puller was winding down and he was ready to make a life move. So he moved out. I was a huge Lifter Puller fan. I really loved them. There's a live recording of them where you can hear me shouting in the background when they played at Brownies.

GALEN POLIVKA: I'd been in New York six, seven years. I moved here with childhood friends of mine. I was playing in some capacity the whole time. Nothing that really took off, but it was so satisfying and exciting to be a musician in New York and see everything going on. Which is why I moved here—the stimuli of it and everything else. I kept tabs on Lifter Puller and we'd see them when they played New York. I was always a fan, and anything that Craig's going to get to do is going to be interesting. I just wanted to be involved. And then, six months later, he gave me a call. We started playing with a drummer who, for whatever reason, just didn't work. And I suggested getting Judd.

JUDD COUNSELL: So when I caught wind that Galen and Craig were playing together, it piqued my interest; it sounded like it could be an awesome band. Galen floated the idea by me: would I be interested in coming over and jamming? And I was really into the idea.

GALEN POLIVKA: And then simultaneously, Craig got ahold of Tad again, who was living in LA. And he just came out: "Craig's in? I'm in." And then it just snowballed from there.

TAD KUBLER (GUITAR PLAYER, THE HOLD STEADY): I moved to LA briefly. I was out there for about a year. And then I was in the process of figuring out how I was going to move to New York.

I ended up joining this band Song of Zarathustra and we made a record and then did a six-week tour of Europe and the UK. Very punk rock. Squats. It was gnarly. At the time, I was fucking miserable. But I'm glad I did it. It was great. It was a good experience. And then my girlfriend at the time, Sacha, she's from New York, and she had moved out to LA, and then I helped move her back to New York. Drove cross-country.

CRAIG FINN: He came out to New York and moved in with her, must have been the summer of '02.

TAD KUBLER: And when I was there, I hung out with Craig for the first time since the band. And it was fun. He seemed more relaxed in New York, in a way that he was not in Minneapolis. Craig can be kind of high strung in a lot of ways—we all can, I guess, but Craig's intense. But there was an ease in spending time with him in New York that I had not experienced before. And I started going out more frequently to New York. And every time I did, we hung out more and more.

CRAIG FINN: So Galen and I were trying to get something going on. Tad showed up and was hanging out. Tad could play riffs, you know, before we could even start playing real songs.

JUDD COUNSELL: Tad was the spark that took this thing to the next level. He had a lot of classic rock chops.

CRAIG FINN: Meanwhile, this guy got in touch; his name was Josh Perilo. He had a comedy troupe called Mr. Ass, and he was trying to do a variety show. He was a Lifter Puller fan, and he said, "Can I take you out to dinner?" So we went to this Indian restaurant. He started pitching me the idea of a house band for his comedy troupe, and we would play bumper music: the skit would end and you'd do thirty seconds of "Back in Black," and then as they reassembled for a new skit, you would stop.

TAD KUBLER: At some point, he was like, "You know, these guys from Upright Citizens Brigade have this side-project thing and they want a live rock band, kind of like Paul Shaffer to David Letterman, but it's all rock songs, which is kind of your wheelhouse. Would you want to do this?" Fucking yeah. But I was a little apprehensive to play music with Craig again. It really felt like he pulled the plug on Lifter Puller prematurely. I totally understand why, especially in hindsight. So we just kind of started hanging out. And I think because we had a goal—the very specific intention was to learn the songs to do this thing—it made it really easy. It wasn't like when you start a band and you're trying to write songs, and it's like, "Is this good?" Learning those songs that we did for the UCB guys definitely helped give us kind of this cohesive direction almost without being very deliberate.

CRAIG FINN: This thing was in a bar, Arlene's Grocery, a bar and rock venue on the Lower East Side. During the show, each of the four members would take lead vocal on a cover. "If You Want Blood" was one. There was a lot of hard rock. What was that David Bowie song? "Moonage Daydream." "Are You Ready for the Sex Girls" from *Revenge of the Nerds* was one. Well, it wasn't as good. But it was all fun. Tad was great at it. He would know the riff. I was pretty much worthless. I'm the guy who barely needed to be there because I was playing rhythm guitar and there wasn't really vocals to this stuff, and if there was, I wasn't singing.

TAD KUBLER: I'm sure Craig would tell you this too, that musically he's not always the most dexterous person, because it's just not the school that he comes from. But he was still an integral part of it, because he's the producer, in a way. He's making the schedule and keeping everybody on task. And a lot of times Craig will have the patience and foresight. He's the lead singer because he has the overall vision. He has the will to make it into something. Without Craig, nothing happens, nothing gets done.

CRAIG FINN: So we did it, and it was fun. I think the second one, I think they said, "Do you want to play a song to start?" I'd been writing songs and I showed the guys "Knuckles." So we played that. It was a lot of fun, but after two of them we wanted to start writing our own songs. The other thing was, I'd come up through indie and punk, and as I got to be in my later twenties,

THE MUSIC WE HAD IN COMMON WAS THIN LIZZY, AC/DC, ZEPPELIN

on the Lifter Puller tours we started listening to a lot more classic rock, '70s rock, which I wasn't unaware of totally, but I didn't know the difference between *Let It Bleed* and *Beggar's Banquet*. There was this re-diving into '70s rock and at the same time being a little sick of indie—the attitudes, the people. As Lifter Puller toured, we liked chaos. We thought the Rolling Stones seemed more fun than some of the indie bands and indie people. And the thing was, Tad had such a great guitar tone, and could play these Thin Lizzy riffs. What if we had a band that was like that?

TAD KUBLER: I don't think Craig grew up with rock and roll the same way I did. He discovered a lot of that stuff as an adult, probably. I think it was really refreshing for him coming from a rigid indie rock scene. Just playing rock and roll like that, in a very traditional sense, was . . . *liberating* might be too strong a word. But it was relaxed. It was fun again. So Craig is like, "This is really fun. I'm having a blast. What if we throw out some of our own songs and just let this inform where we go?" And I was like, "Yeah, okay." A lot of it was us sitting in this kitchen over on Pacific and Nevins, in his first apartment, a garden-level apartment. I was literally sitting at a table with an electric guitar not plugged in. And he was pacing back and forth, waving his arms around.

GALEN POLIVKA: I was a latecomer to that bombastic hard rock stuff, because my older brother gave me the gateway drug of Elvis Costello and new wave. I was a thirteen-year-old punk rock reactionary: anything that was on the radio was bullshit. And then at nineteen, you can't *not* hear Led Zeppelin growing up in America. You hear *Physical Graffiti* when you're nineteen with new ears, and it's, *Oh, why, why am I supposed to hate this again? That's ridiculous*. I really hate the cliché of, "Oh, man, the people onstage and the audience, we're the same." No, some people are onstage and some people aren't. But it was the opposite of Led Zeppelin. There was no mysticism, just friends of yours playing songs together. It was as straightforward as it sounds, which is appealing.

CRAIG FINN: The music we had in common was Thin Lizzy, AC/DC, Zeppelin. I think those were probably the big three. That's what I remember listening to a lot. We liked Van Halen. And there was indie stuff we all liked. But I think those were the ones. Thin Lizzy was the biggest. I sort of felt it was okay for indie people to admit to liking that stuff, but it wasn't for you to play, you know what I mean? You acknowledged it was what you listened to at high school parties, but it wasn't Sonic Youth-y or noisy enough. It was too basic, too meat-and-potatoes. And I guess that was the power in playing that stuff.

TAD KUBLER: Galen's from Milwaukee but lived in Minneapolis—both Galen and Judd lived there. I hadn't met either of them until we got to New York, which seems weird. Anybody who's met Galen would say he's one of the most affable people you'll ever meet. He just seemed like a nice dude. And Judd was the Will Ferrell of rock and roll. He was a walking party, but not necessarily in a drugs-and-alcohol way. He's just constantly pumped up. He got pulled over once for air-drumming. Rush came on the radio, and I guess he just went berserk.

JUDD COUNSELL: That is a true story. I was riding in my parents' minivan with Galen, driving down Lake Drive, which is the main street in Milwaukee. We were listening to Rush and I was air-drumming, doing the "Tom Sawyer" fill. After a while I noticed there were lights in the rearview. I pulled over and a cop came over. He was furious because he had been following me for miles with lights on and I had no idea, because I was listening to Rush.

TAD KUBLER: Playing with those guys was really easy. And given the style we were chasing, I was interested in how it was going to work with what Craig does, because that is very specific, and it can be polarizing. The great thing about it is that there's no question who you're listening to. You know it's Craig immediately. But it was just fun. And it didn't seem serious.

GALEN POLIVKA: Our first practice space had a bar in it, which is very Hold Steady, come to think of it. It was small, but it was a proper bar. And there was a kegerator, as they say in the Midwest. So that didn't always help productivity, but it was there. We just had chemistry right away. When you're coming up with new stuff on a pretty prolific level, it's exciting. You want to keep that ball rolling, and riffs were just like jumping out of Tad. So it was, "Let's fucking get in the space and figure them out." When you're kicking ass, it's fun, and you want to continue kicking ass.

CRAIG FINN: It was never a chore to practice because we were gonna get a bunch of beer and have a party with the instruments on. After moving to New York and spending two years not playing loud guitar, to have a practice space where we could have guitars and drums and a bunch of beer and a bottle of whiskey? It all fed into each other. It was a fun band because we were having fun.

JUDD COUNSELL: We were all wary of starting a new band, but we all liked playing. We just backed into it. Craig was prolific, he had songs. "Oh, we'll play those." Then Tad would bring stuff, so we'd do that. And it just kept building. But the premise was that it would always be a bar band, not something we would pursue.

GALEN POLIVKA: Musically it was a really tight fit—it felt good pretty quickly. It wasn't a concept or anything, but Craig's demeanor being what it is, and his whole vibe being what it is like, having this bludgeoning, ham-fisted rock band behind that is the last thing you'd expect. Our style happened super organically and there was a lack of preciousness to it. And it's an interesting dynamic too: it's not one guy with an acoustic guitar going, *Blah, blah, blah, here's the vocal melody and here's what I have in mind for arrangements*. It's two separate people coming at it, and that leads it to be just more wide open, because there's already compromise. It was pretty straightforward. We just literally got into a basement and bashed stuff out for fun. And then it turned into something that lasted twenty years.

SYD BUTLER (BASSIST, 8G BAND/*LATE NIGHT WITH SETH MEYERS*, LES SAVY FAV; PRESIDENT, FRENCHKISS RECORDS): Years ago, Les Savy Fav was on tour with a band called Girls Against Boys. We played in Minneapolis and we met Craig and Tad, who were in Lifter Puller, or LFTR PLLR. We played really early, as the opening band, and they were the only people in the audience. Tad generously gave us a place to stay afterward, and they were so kind, so we stayed in touch. Later

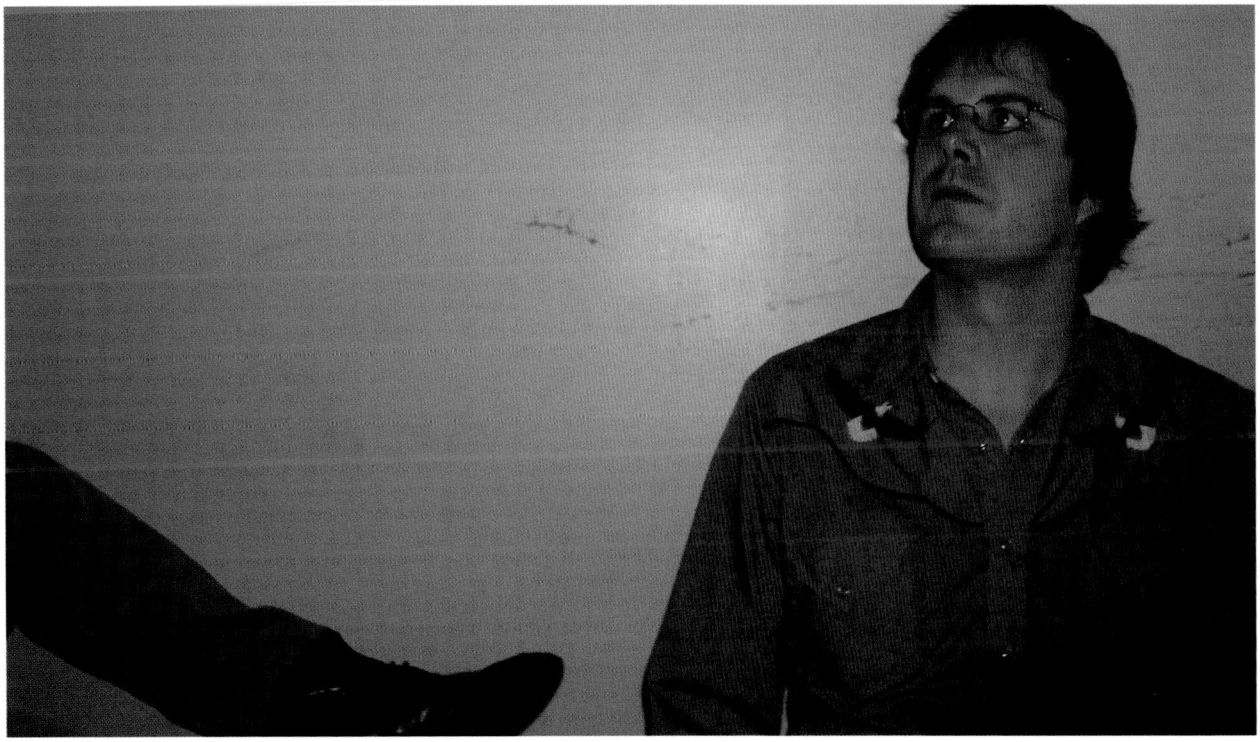

on, Lifter Puller asked Frenchkiss to put out a record—it was our second or third release—and we loved it and we loved those guys to death. Then Craig moved to New York. He told me, "I'm starting a bar band called The Hold Steady. We're not going to be able to tour. We're just going to play local bars for something to do." We went out and got a burrito, and I said, "Anything you record, I will put out."

CRAIG FINN: We started writing songs, and then I thought, *Let's go record them.* I think when we recorded the first six songs, the engineer was like, "This is good." And then our friend Steve Koester had a show at Northsix in Williamsburg, and he was looking for a support. This was early 2003, the end of January. Meanwhile, Lifter Puller had weirdly gotten a lot bigger on the Internet. There was a strange article that came out in the *Village Voice* for no reason. I open it up one day and there's a full-page article on Lifter Puller and I don't know why. There was stuff like that happening, and so when we did play this first show, it wasn't packed, but for a first show . . . the cap is 400, maybe, and there were 100 there, 150. Pretty good. And people we didn't know were there. It wasn't like your friends from work. It was like, "These guys are coming to see the new Lifter Puller thing." And that was a success at some level. And almost immediately after that, some of the indie labels got in touch.

JUDD COUNSELL: I think the first show was with Koester and the Wrens. We were the first band, and we played our set, and I remember Steve Koester coming up after: "Whoa, that was really good—but how am I going to follow that?" Because he was a quiet singer-songwriter and we just came out and melted faces. That was the first moment where we truly thought we might have something, just seeing the responses of people there.

GALEN POLIVKA: I remember there being far more people there than I thought there were going to be. I would guesstimate there were more than a hundred people there, but not much more. We were psyched. Lifter Puller definitely had momentum going before they broke up, so that helped, obviously. But just to be met with some kind of enthusiasm off the bat was really exciting.

TAD KUBLER: Because of the way Lifter Puller ended and the rise of the Internet, I think we reached so many more people. It seemed like we kind of had a built-in audience right away. And that was bizarre and incredibly fortunate. Craig's delivery and his style and everything about him allowed us to really sidestep the gimmicky stuff like some of those bands that were doing the classic rock thing, but you couldn't tell if it was ironic.

CRAIG FINN: I think most people got it, but for the first few years, I remember people saying

it took them a second to understand whether this was an ironic presentation, like the Darkness or something. I think the way we presented it helped—T-shirts and jeans, no dressing up—but there were a few people that were, "Whoa!" I remember having a graphic designer present something that I thought was very overly '70s, and I said, "No, we're not going to do anything like that, not push it too far in that direction." There was always a managing of the imagery to make sure it wasn't too campy.

TAD KUBLER: We definitely felt very separate from the Brooklyn bands, in that we were celebrating some of the more traditional things in rock and roll. Especially making the first two records, we weren't afraid to look like we were trying.

CRAIG FINN: "Positive Jam" was in your face, to have that lead-up of all the decades, and then Tad comes in. People are going to have to make a decision: if we are going to open with this song—and we can't put it in the middle of the set—it's going to be one way or the other. People might be repulsed. We probably had seven songs before that, because that song debuted at our second or third show. But I remember that one was, "We've got something here."

GALEN POLIVKA: If there was anything we were pushing against, it was the elitism of the indie rock stuff of the early '90s. There's nothing wrong with being smart, obviously. But some people would beat you over the head with it. And it just got a little clever. Anything rockist was considered wildly uncool, and arbitrary people just dictating what's cool and what isn't cool doesn't sit well.

CRAIG FINN: Our crowd was indie. It was people our age—thirties. And people who were coming out of indie stuff. Even though we were playing that music, and everyone was familiar with it from driving round smoking weed in high school, it was indie people. Les Savy Fav was the band we were hanging out with; Tad was living right below [singer] Tim Harrington. We were going to all their shows, we were very connected with them, socially and otherwise. Even though that seems musically way different, it was almost the same audience.

SYD BUTLER: We were all very tight. I would see Craig a lot. We lived half a mile from each other.

DEAN BALTULONIS (COPRODUCER, ***ALMOST KILLED ME, SEPARATION SUNDAY,*** AND ***HEAVEN IS WHENEVER***): That was the time when bands like TV on the Radio and Yeah Yeah Yeahs were the Brooklyn sound. And these guys are going in the exact opposite direction and doing bar rock, which no one was doing.

IF THERE WAS ANYTHING WE WERE PUSHING AGAINST, IT WAS THE ELITISM OF THE INDIE ROCK STUFF OF THE EARLY '90S

CRAIG FINN: I definitely didn't feel part of a Brooklyn scene. But the Favs were always a weird band to me. They felt like a very important Brooklyn band, but they were just before. We felt connected to them, but not to the Strokes or the other Strokes-esque bands. The Wrens, we played their record release at the Bowery Ballroom and that felt like a big show for us. We didn't really feel connected with other stuff that was getting a lot of notice.

SYD BUTLER: They weren't Interpol or Yeah Yeah Yeahs or the Strokes. They did not fit there. Les Savy Fav fit more in that space. But they fit in a different realm of people that didn't know about the Strokes and Yeah Yeah Yeahs. They fit with—I don't know if this sounds right—an educated, working-class audience that didn't feel comfortable with the angular haircut bands. They connected with people who went to work and liked to watch a rock band. And that was a great place for them to be. They were on the edge of things—they could play with one of those bands like the Strokes, but then be fine playing in a bar, drinking beer and playing rock.

TAD KUBLER: We knew this should kick ass. This is something that I've thought a lot about, because you hear it kind of used to define traditional rock bands a lot, especially classic rock bands: we wanted to be able to do that without being overly male or macho. I certainly wouldn't describe any of us as macho guys. Bobby's probably the closest. He's kind of like the Marlboro Man a little bit. He'll get in the hot tub with his jeans on.

CRAIG FINN: *The Last Waltz*, when it was reissued, my ex-wife took me to see it in a theater. And I said, "I don't think I'm gonna like this." I knew almost zero going into that movie about the Band. I knew the big three songs. But I didn't know they looked cool, I didn't know they *were* cool. I didn't know they hung out with Bob Dylan. I knew nothing. I certainly didn't know Van Morrison was going to do that performance. All of it was very exciting. And so when I got the DVD, Tad and

I watched it and loved it. But a lot of it was also just drinking beer and reconnecting on this less indie, more rock-music basis. The Truckers's show was very big. I remember that as being one of the greatest shows I'd ever seen.

Some guys at the company I worked with, DCN, were more into alt-country stuff, stuff I thought was okay but wasn't really my thing. They would talk about Drive-By Truckers all the time and quote them and eventually I spun *Southern Rock Opera*. All the talking, I loved, all the vamping and talking and the storytelling. And then I went to see them, and they were really on a high. I think it was their first time at the Bowery Ballroom level, first time they were drawing five hundred people, and they were drinking whiskey from the bottle, and it looked like they were having a blast. It felt like I could do this, *we* could do this. It looked really fun. It was looser in a way than anything indie is, and I think that was something I wanted to do.

With any band, musically, if I play this part, then you play this part, then we both do it at the same time, we'll end up at the same place. It's like synchronized swimming. It's like marching in lockstep. And because of the Truckers, I became interested in bands that keep the structures a little looser, which we did some, so there's a little more of a ride to take together during the show, and you see that in different songs in our set. That was coming from a limited musician, and that was a big breakthrough of what I wanted to do. I thought that would make things more entertaining night to night internally, meaning if we can't totally control who's going to show up, maybe it could be musically transcendent in some way, in a way a lot of indie can't be, because it doesn't allow for any improvisation or structural differences.

TAD KUBLER: I do remember talking to Craig about the Drive-By Truckers show, and how energized he was by it. It went beyond just the music. He was like, "Yeah, man, the lead singer is drinking wine onstage. I should do that." I was like, "That would be a fucking disaster. I mean, two songs in and you'd be covered in red wine."

The *Last Waltz* thing is also true. We watched it on DVD at his apartment, accompanied by a tremendous amount of beer. It was two guys being like, "Oh, man, I'll rewind that part." I watched it seeing not just the joy, but how there was a fluidity to it, and part of that speaks to the caliber of players. The part that we took away from it was these guys were listening to each other; they're not just going up and regurgitating this thing that they've rehearsed. It's almost like it has its own life to it, that they're participating in, rather than just showing you this performance they've rehearsed.

Those were certainly two big things. *The Last Waltz* was the initial one. And then that Truckers show, I think, came later, because we'd had our first few shows. Our first couple of shows, I remember being really nervous and really wound up and almost in a panic that I wasn't going to be able to get enough booze in me to relax and be able to play. So I stepped into a liquor store, and I got probably a dozen or so of those little airline bottles of whiskey and vodka. And I just lined them

up on top of my amp. And I would bang away at them—over the course of thirty minutes. That lasted for a while—I don't remember how many shows, but far too many. And I think that's where the wine thing came in with the Truckers. Craig was like, "I need a thing like that." I was like, "Maybe I'll do the wine and you should do the airline bottles. They have a top on them, at least."

JUDD COUNSELL: Tad would have airplane bottles and it would be hilarious. But then he would drink them and not remember what happened later in the night. Even Tad after a while felt he couldn't do the airplane thing every night, because he was waking up in strange places.

CRAIG FINN: I could tell people liked it and were kind of amused by it. You know, "What is this? Holy shit."

SYD BUTLER: I thought they had dialed into something magical; I couldn't believe the guy I loved from Lifter Puller had captured this Springsteen feel. Tad played bass in Lifter Puller, and all of a sudden he's playing guitar and they're pulling out all this classic rock stuff, with this madman creature out front. It was both refreshing and familiar . . . it felt quite revolutionary.

CRAIG FINN: Tad was unhinged at this point. He was, to be honest, drinking *a lot.* He had this massive amp called a Park, it was the loudest amp I think that has ever been created.

GALEN POLIVKA: It was like the monolith in 2001—the chimps are frolicking around it and crushing skulls. I'm not a gear person; it was insanely loud, though. It was a half stack, but it

I WANTED TO CREATE NOT QUITE CHAOS, BUT AN INTERACTION WITH THE AUDIENCE THAT MIGHT INVOLVE CHAOS

was ungodly loud. Everybody had to turn up to compensate. It was pretty ludicrous considering the rooms we were playing. Friends of ours who were musicians would come to the shows and just be like, "Dude, Tad's amp is completely out of control." The attitude was, "I'm just gonna turn it up as loud as it goes and see what happens." Which can be endearing or kind of punishing. It was mythically loud, especially for how comparatively compact it was. He was not Kevin Shields, he was just a dude in a club.

TAD KUBLER: Yeah, that was absurd. I remember being indignant when sound guys would say, "Dude, you've got to turn down!" I'd be like, "What do *you* know? What's the problem?" It was rated 100 watts, but I think it ran at about 120 or 115. They invented those amps to play stadiums before they had PA systems. The two amps I use onstage now are both less than fifteen watts and they're too loud. It was absurd. That those guys even speak to me still is somewhat of a miracle and speaks to their compassion. So yeah, *unhinged* would be the way I would describe it too, for the record.

CRAIG FINN: At the end of Lifter Puller we played a lot of shows with Dillinger Four in Minneapolis. And their shows were chaotic, and sometimes drunk to the point where it wasn't great, but their fans loved them. It was like the Replacements: the fans loved them; whatever they were going to get, they loved it. And I wanted to try to build something like that. *It's gonna be a tightrope act some nights, but we're not going to be boring.* Eventually I came to embrace the boring, as most bands do. I think we may have loaded out Tad that night more than his amp. But he was wailing on guitar, and it was just the four of us, and it was very good. And people seemed to really like it.

TAD KUBLER: Did Craig tell you the story about the first Baltimore show?

CRAIG FINN: My good friend Roman Kuebler—no relation to Tad—was at our first show. And he owned a little club down in Baltimore, and he said, "We got a gig, my band's playing, you got to come down and play." So a couple weeks later, we were down in Baltimore playing to a filled club on a Saturday night. That show a few people flew in for who were Lifter Puller fans and wanted to see the new band. Again, we were drafting off the Lifter Puller thing a little bit, and that show went really well and was also very chaotic. We were shotgunning beers onstage and throwing empty cans. It was non-indie behavior. It was embracing a certain Midwesternness too.

TAD KUBLER: Judd and Galen hadn't spent a lot of time with me at this point. Craig had certainly put the time in, he was certified. I got super wasted before the show, to the point of semi–passing out in the van. Judd and Galen were like, "This is a disaster! We're fucked! Are we even gonna play the show?" Craig was like, "Don't worry about it. Just fucking put a guitar on him and point him toward the stage and everything will be fine." Which is what happened. Both Judd and Galen were like, "What the fuck is going on here?" I think they were terrified.

I wanted to create not quite chaos, but an interaction with the audience that might involve chaos, and eventually the stage invasions and everything. The encouragement of drunkenness. My goal in all that wasn't to get super wasted. It was to break down the barriers between the audience and myself, so we're on the same level, and I'm totally wasted too. Especially in the early days, there was a creeping feeling that this is all going to go away, that it's going to end tomorrow, so we better enjoy this *now*. Because it might not be happening in six months. I think that was a big part of all the things like stage invasions and the shenanigans that surrounded the band for the first five years.

CRAIG FINN: Being Midwestern was something that made us unique. It was just taking a contrarian position always. Yes, there are probably going to be bands from the Midwest who moved to Brooklyn six months ago and they're wearing leather. We moved here two years ago, and we're from Minneapolis, and I would wear Minnesota Twins stuff all the time. There hadn't been a popular band there since the Replacements or Soul Asylum. It had been a good ten years. Not many people knew that much about it, so there was something to explore there that you could reinvent without people saying, "That's not right."

TWO

SO MANY SHOWS WHERE NOBODY COMES OUT

BY ROB SHEFFIELD

JANUARY 2004: AN ARCTIC SATURDAY NIGHT IN BROOKLYN. WE'RE shivering in the back of Northsix, waiting to see Les Savy Fav. We've also got tickets to see the Stills at Bowery Ballroom tonight, an excellent band from Montreal, but my girlfriend's obsessed

with Les Savy Fav, so here we are. It's so nightmarishly freezing, we linger long over dinner and make a point of getting here at midnight, to skip the opening act. We groan aloud when four dudes come out to set up. None of them are bearded, which means it's not Les Savy Fav. Damn. The opening band.

But these guys crack me up just plugging in. They do not resemble an NYC band circa 2004, a time and place where most people are DJs. Not a skinny tie in sight. Nary a sullen pout. In their tennis shirts and slacks, they seem more like a pickup whiffle-ball team of tipsy paralegals. In fact, we're not sure they're actually the band until they start to play an eerie tale about North American history in the twentieth century. By the end of the song, it's clear this song is called "Positive Jam," and the band is The Hold Steady. They've got my attention, but I have to admit a few questions cross my mind: Are they kidding? Is this a gag? Isn't this a lot of concept to lay on a sea of semi-hostile strangers' faces, one of which is mine?

Tough to pinpoint the exact moment it goes from "weird" to "brilliant" to "best thing ever" for me. The song where the girl gets a bloody nose from sniffing margarita mix? The creepy spiderweb story with Sunny D vs. Five Alive? For my girlfriend, it's the pickle chips. But the way I remember it, the second song is "The Swish," and the one-two punch makes mincemeat out of me. By the doomy opening riff of "Killer Parties," I've got a new favorite band.

Way too cold for slices after the show, but we go to Anna Maria Pizza anyway, just to rave over what we just saw. I keep thinking, *Thank God we didn't go see the Stills tonight.* (Love that band, especially *Logic Will Break Your Heart*, but we find The Hold Steady and she eventually marries me, so I'd call it a successful Saturday night.)

The Hold Steady keep playing out—Northsix, Warsaw, Bowery, Mercury Lounge—even if it's

just a handful of believers. "There are seventeen people here," Ally whispers one night at Northsix. "I'm the only girl." (One out of seventeen wasn't a bad ratio in those days.) *Mouths and hands, baby, hands and mouths. So many shows where nobody comes out.*

But every show feels like a revelation. When the guitars get jovial, the stories get grim. When the stories get grim, the guitars get jovial. Tad puts a punk twist on his '70s burnout guitar riffs, with so much unironic gusto it's terrifying. Galen powers each song with his thunderthud bass groove.

Frantically scribbling lyrics in my pocket notebook, so I'll remember the next day. Trying to guess the song titles. (Now *that* was a waste of time.) Reaching into the speakers, trying to hold on to the quarter notes. Desperately waiting for the next chance to hear these songs again.

One night in May, they play "Milkcrate Mosh." Craig tells a couple dozen fans at Bowery about the night he saw a guy at a hardcore show wearing a milk crate on his head, because he was here to kick it "old-school Boston style." Craig adds, "I had no idea what he meant—but I REALLY wanted to kick it old-school Boston style." What a groove: an alternate universe where CCR's "Susie Q" and PiL's "Albatross" are the same song? Close enough. Total strangers making eye contact in that "Did he just say that?" way. Buying the "Milkcrate Mosh" 7-inch from Craig at the merch table, but not saying hi. (Too shy.) Playing the single constantly. (The B side: "Hey, Hey What Can I Do." Playing it once.)

They release their CD that spring: *The Hold Steady Almost Killed Me*. (That's the title to me, in the tradition of *Ramones Leave Home* or *The Beach Boys Love You*. Always dislike the three-word abbreviation. I'm probably just wrong.) Listening on the iPod, walking nose-first into a lamppost at Bedford and North 10th because I'm laughing too hard to see straight. (The line: "*A ray of light in white rayon slacks*.") I rave about this genius album in *Rolling Stone*, where the fact-checkers change "Tusken Raiders" to "Tuscan Raiders." Feels symbolic, somehow.

But the new songs keep coming. A hot August night, Bowery almost full this time, Craig asks, "You know those ads on the subway that say 1-212-Margarita?" We all do—it's the hotline of a personal-injury lawyer. He turns the L train ad into a girl, then turns the girl into a song. It's an election year, so Craig announces, "You know who I'll vote for? Anyone who passes a law against people eating on the subway." But this election year goes wrong, on every possible level. November 4 at Northsix, two nights after Election Day, hardly a soul in the room. We're an audience of zombies, everyone too depressed to move. Craig mentions another dismal bit of news—back in Minneapolis, the First Avenue club just announced they're closing. The song they dedicate: "Certain Songs."

Every gig has a different vibe. The first one that's sold out? March 2005 at Mercury Lounge. On the sidewalk, I meet a cheerful guy from Maine; he doesn't have a ticket, but he just drove across four state lines to see if he can bluff his way in. He tells me it's the first rock show he's gone to in years; he heard this band on a blog and just KNEW. Not gonna lie, he freaks me out a bit—probably freaks out the bouncers too, because they let him in. I don't realize it yet, but I'm going to be meeting a lot of this guy over the next few years at Hold Steady shows.

They play a bunch of new songs that night, so scribbling down lyrics faster than ever—did he really just rhyme "William Butler Yeats" with "summer 1988"? Yes, he did. *Separation Sunday* comes out. A double take at the cover photo—hey, that's the corner of Conselyea and Maspeth in

Williamsburg. Right next to that tiny grotto shrine to Our Lady of Lourdes, hidden away behind the White Castle. (The White Castle is long gone, but the grotto's still there.)

Sitting in Hi-Fi with the band, August 2005, watching the TV over the bar as they play "Your Little Hoodrat Friend" on *Conan*. Their first late-night TV gig. They're so nervous for the first minute or so, until the switch flips at "*Damn right she'll rise again.*" Franz dancing at the piano. The exhilaration on Bobby's face. Telling Tad my sappy but sincere joy at seeing this band start to get the attention they deserve. Tad shakes his head and says, "Now I'm just waiting for the backlash."

The first show that's scary? Easy—April 2006, Warsaw, with Les Savy Fav, total chaos. They keep begging the kids to take a step back. Loads of new songs that night; a bunch of them sound like .38 Special. Visiting the Dumbo studio where they're cutting the new album, seeing Franz and Galen taking a break in the van outside. I tell them how much I dig the .38 Special songs. They laugh, open the glove box, hand me a cassette bought at a highway truck stop: .38 Special's greatest hits. Watching Craig cut the vocal for "First Night." Hearing Tad play Jefferson Starship's "Find Your Way Back" over and over.

The first show where I see Tad bust out the double-neck Gibson? October 2006, at Irving Plaza. Craig: "The next time we play here, Tad will have purchased Aleister Crowley's castle." The first time they don't play "Killer Parties"? June 2008, at McCarren Pool, in a thunderstorm. They've reached the point where they have too many bangers to fit them all in the set. Tad's birthday, so during "Resurrection," Craig says, "Tad, I'm giving you the gift of soloing." His solo is so ramshackle, it's downright poignant. Another big first at that show: where the hell did all these kids in matching *Unified Scene* shirts come from?

Interviewing Iggy Pop, asking him if he's ever heard The Hold Steady. He apologizes, says he never listens to new bands, but people keep telling him about this one. I ask if he's heard the song that begins, "*Me and my friends are like / The drums on 'Lust for Life.'*" Iggy made me repeat that three times, just to get it straight. He says, "I haven't heard the song . . . but I wish I had friends like that."

The first show where we all realize this isn't our local bar band anymore? Webster Hall, December 2005. The big homecoming show, after they've traveled the world for *Separation Sunday*. They tell a funny story about playing a high school that had a Hold Steady dress-alike contest, which naturally turned into a Franz dress-alike contest. But they haven't played NYC in months, which feels like forever. They belong to the world now. A turning point and everyone knows it—a triumph, really. I've never felt "Killer Parties" so deeply. I scrawl a sentence in my notebook about how when we die, we'll all turn into songs, and hear each other and remember each other. Backstage, after the show, Craig says how weird it felt to sing "*Oh, to be thirty-three forever*" for the last time in 2005. Hell, next year he'll be thirty-four.

So many Hold Steady shows since then—I gave up counting after the first few dozen, but way more than I've seen any other band. Yet every show turns into a story. I never go to a Hold Steady show without hearing people tell their stories about some other Hold Steady show. In a crucial way, trading our stories is part of the show. Sometimes you might even wonder if we go to the shows for the stories.

But it's more like this: the show is what happens when we come together to be part of a story.

Every fan has their own stories, their own songs, the favorites we cling to like patron saints. The deep cut you pray for live. The song you pick as your designated bathroom break. ("Magazines.") The song you never fucking hear, not even once: "Curves and Nerves," my white whale. One of my favorites, a song that knocks me flat and buries me in a shallow grave, with a Nazareth tape and a vodka ice and Gatorade. Yet I've never heard it live, beyond a rough take at a sound check. We've all got those.

But the shows get scratched into our souls, and so do the stories. We mix our own mythologies, dictate our own doxologies, try out our new testaments on the guys sitting next to us at the bar. I think about these stories whenever I'm walking to the next show, which for me is usually Brooklyn Bowl. Right down the street from Northsix, which changed its name to Music Hall of Williamsburg. It's the same walk as in 2004, down the same stretch of Greenpoint, along the East River. Past the tiny cobbler shop that Craig sings about in "Meserole," one of his lost solo classics ("*Manhattan Ave. and Meserole, zippers fixed and boots resoled*"), a song about the sheer radical weirdness of repairing broken things instead of giving up and throwing them away. (The shop is still there, BTW. So is First Avenue.)

How many nights have I taken that same walk-on-back along the river to hear this same band? So many nights. Never enough of them.

Rob Sheffield is a longtime writer for Rolling Stone. *His books include* Love Is a Mix Tape, Talking to Girls About Duran Duran, *and* Dreaming the Beatles: The Love Story of One Band and the Whole World.

THREE

NO OVERTHINKING THE CHORDS

TAD KUBLER: *Almost Killed Me* was literally written by me and Craig in his kitchen.

CRAIG FINN: When I moved away from Minneapolis, I got to look back and see what was unique about it and think about that a lot. Also, there was the Truckers thing, getting into their music and thinking, *They tell all these stories about the people in Alabama and Mississippi. What if we made where we're from the center of our universe and tried to tell those stories?* Also, there was a sense with this posturing and posing that I ascribe to the indie rock of the New York scene of the moment, the hi-hat rock, being really honest about where you're from and who you are and your age and your weight, it seemed like there was a lot of power in that to me. And I wanted to work with that.

JUDD COUNSELL: One of the great things about working with The Hold Steady was we really didn't overthink things. We rehearsed and we went in and recorded almost live. Early on we were doing "Hot Fries," and I remember all of us laughing at Craig's lyric, because we'd never actually heard it properly before we went to the studio—you couldn't hear it in a rehearsal space. We really had a set-'em-up-and-knock-'em-down mentality, which was great for the band.

CRAIG FINN: Holly, Gideon, and Charlemagne emerged as characters first on *Almost Killed Me*. I listened back to "Slip Sliding Away" by Paul Simon, and about halfway through that verse he says, *"Delores, I live in fear."* My parents had that record, and dropping a woman's proper name in the middle of a verse became something I would do at the end of Lifter Puller. But I started to develop these characters through the songs during *Almost Killed Me*, without fleshing them out. They were ideas getting sketched out, almost, at first. I had a lot of confidence: in Minneapolis coming out of Lifter Puller, people were quoting lyrics and hosting costume parties based on the characters. So I knew I could get through to some people, and I was pretty confident about the writing.

TAD KUBLER: A lot of the songs on *Almost Killed Me*, Craig would have the initial sense of what it should be. That was the hardest record, almost, especially because my only other experience writing with Craig was Lifter Puller, which was so different, and where I played bass. I would try to interpret where I either knew Craig wanted to go or where I thought he wanted to go.

"HEY, IF I'M NOT SINGING, JUST RIP A SOLO." THE GUITAR SOLO ITSELF IN 2002 WAS SORT OF OBNOXIOUS IN A PUNK ROCK WAY.

DEAN BALTULONIS: I had a studio in Brooklyn called Atomic Recording Company. And one of the partners grew up with Craig. His name was Matt Henderson. He was working on a solo album with Craig—this was pre–Hold Steady. They brought me in to work on that album with them. That had a lot of the characters that morphed into The Hold Steady's first record. That's how I met Craig. And from Craig, I met Tad. We all lived in the same neighborhood in Brooklyn. So we started hanging out together, going to bars, and became pretty close friends. That morphed into the demos for *Almost Killed Me*, which actually became the first session. We recorded half the record in one session, and then Frenchkiss picked it up, and we went back and finished the record.

SYD BUTLER: Frenchkiss comes from a place of the artist. I saw there was a spark there. And Frenchkiss loves signing bands at the beginning of their career—that's the exciting part. I trusted Craig and his ability to be exceptional. I knew there was greatness there.

FRANZ NICOLAY (KEYBOARD PLAYER, THE HOLD STEADY): I met Craig after Lifter Puller had broken up, when he had moved to New York and was working for Digital Club Network, DCN, which was a dot-com, an early arts dot-com. They were putting cameras on the roofs of clubs and trying to livestream concerts. It wasn't really working that well because nobody at that point had high-speed Internet at home. But that was his gig. They decided they were going to branch out into doing live records, and that's how I met Craig—he was sort of the A&R guy for a World/Inferno live record, and I was the point person for the band on that project, so we ended up working together. That was about the time that he had started putting The Hold Steady together, and he asked me and Peter, one of the sax players from World/Inferno, to come and play on the record that became *Almost Killed Me*.

TAD KUBLER: We initially had Franz come in to play "Certain Songs." It sounded so good that I said we should have him do something else, and "Sweet Payne" was the obvious one. I took a piece of paper and wrote down the different chords that were in the song and then sat in the live room while he played the piano and pointed to which chords were coming up next. And it sounded good.

FRANZ NICOLAY: My first impression was that the lyrics were great—it seemed like a continuation of Lifter Puller in many ways. The music I remember being not as excited about. There were people who first heard The Hold Steady and weren't that excited about it. I basically shared that impression, which was that it was derivative of classic rock. It wasn't as exciting as Lifter Puller. I was doing a lot of that kind of work at that point, coming in and playing on other people's records, and this was the same. I knew I was going to play on "You Gotta Dance" and "Modesto" and "Certain Songs" and "Hostile," and once I was there, Tad was like, "Oh, you could play on this other one, 'Sweet Payne,'" and I couldn't wrap my brain around the form of it, so what we ended up doing was just listing all the chords that were in the song on a piece of paper, and he stood next to me with a pair of headphones in the control room and pointed with a pencil at what chord was coming up.

CRAIG FINN: Thinking about that first Replacements record, which is a favorite of mine, when Paul stops singing, Bobby plays a solo. And that just seems like what our MO was. "Hey, if

I'm not singing, just rip a solo." The guitar solo itself in 2002 was sort of obnoxious in a punk rock way. And it was a particular kind of guitar solo too: Mick Ronson–like, the belligerent guitar solo, not the well-crafted, studied one. It was just playing a blues scale loud with the amp turned up. Some of the songs were things I had at least started: "Positive Jam" was something I had. I had it as a faster thing, more of an indie thing, and then we said, "What if it was more of a stand-alone?" and then Tad came up with the Zeppy bit.

"The Swish," Tad showed me the song and I wrote lyrics to it. "Barfruit" was one more like we're talking about: I had lyrics over very basic chords and traditionally in Lifter Puller, we would have made the chords more unique, more unusual. But in this band, it was, "No—these two chords go together, B and F sharp, these are classic, so why overthink it?" A lot of the songwriting choices were about that: "Knuckles" is C to F. It's one to four. Where in indie you have to diminish something or put in a seventh to make it sound gritty, or like it doesn't resolve quite as nicely, but we wanted to do something that was maybe a little comforting. I guess they settled into structures, some of them. But we were a little looser. Just play it again, and when it feels like it should go to the chorus, go to the chorus.

GALEN POLIVKA: It was very collaborative. Craig and Tad came in and different songs were done to varying degrees. When we started there was no sharing of files—it was back to the four-guys-in-a-room thing. It wasn't like, "Oh, here's this idea that I demoed, and it's pretty much done." It was bashed out in the room largely. Tad and Craig did the vast majority of the refining of stuff, though—the majority of the heavy lifting artistically was done by Craig and Tad, for sure.

DEAN BALTULONIS: Lifter Puller had some traction in the States, in the Midwest, so I was excited to work with those guys. But the first half of that record was just demos to give to labels. I think we did the first half of the record in two or three days. And then we finished the record in another two or three days.

CRAIG FINN: In 2003 we went to work and we played shows. Might have played twice in Baltimore. We played some local shows, every month, every six weeks. And then we got the record together. We recorded again sometime in '03, and Frenchkiss signed us. I think Frenchkiss made a big difference, especially back then, and the other thing is, we had a couple offers, but Les Savy Fav were friends of ours. We'd played some shows with them. They put out all this angular indie-punk stuff, and I thought framing our classic rock band, putting it alongside that stuff, would be really good. You'd see it differently. And I think that really worked. I think that got people to pay attention to it in a different way. They saw it as maybe artsier.

TAD KUBLER: I was surprised [Frenchkiss signed the band]. Particularly because we didn't necessarily fit in with the archetype of stuff they were releasing. I was just surprised that people were as excited to hear it as they actually were.

GALEN POLIVKA: Craig and Syd had a rapport already, so it wasn't super surprising, but we were definitely aware of how fortunate it was. I mean, they hadn't heard a note, because there wasn't one yet. That's huge, obviously, and it's encouraging: *Oh shit, like, people believe in this! People think this has wheels before it even really exists!* There was definitely a cachet of cool that we wouldn't have but for Frenchkiss, for sure.

SYD BUTLER: I think we printed three thousand copies and we were hoping we would sell them over a couple of years. The band would go on tour, play rock clubs, and sell a couple CDs a night. And that's not what happened at all. By the end of the year we were racing to repress. It was difficult to keep up with the demand, and the learning curve was steep. I needed a lot of help. I rushed out and hired people with more music business experience. I had to ramp up to a bigger distributor. And everyone was very supportive.

CRAIG FINN: By the time *Almost Killed Me* came out [in March 2004], we may have got a booking agent. We went down to South by Southwest, and that was kind of a dividing thing. When the record came out we had the opportunity to play the Frenchkiss show. We decided we'd go through Minneapolis. We played in Chicago, Minneapolis, I think Des Moines, then straight to Austin and straight home. Judd, I think, had just had a baby and had an advertising career that was going well. He just couldn't do it. As much as we loved him, and he was a great drummer, he couldn't do it.

JUDD COUNSELL: That was the first thing I couldn't do. I loved the band and I was wary of slowing their momentum. Once the band started touring it changed the stakes for me, because what started as a bar band became more of a commitment. I had been in bands for a long time. I'd committed to bands. But I was transitioning to a non-band life—I needed to find an actual job. And at the same time, I couldn't resist playing with The Hold Steady. But once they started moving to that next level, I wasn't prepared to make that commitment—I'd had my first kid. At the time, they would say, "We'll play Minneapolis, so we'll play a week out and then a week back." And then a month later it was the same with South by and I wasn't sure I could do that. So the first South by was Bobby.

OH SHIT, LIKE, PEOPLE BELIEVE IN THIS! PEOPLE THINK THIS HAS WHEELS BEFORE IT EVEN REALLY EXISTS!

CRAIG FINN: I knew Bobby a little bit, but Tad knew him better. Tad said, "Bobby could maybe do it." So we called Bobby. Tad can tell you about the phone call.

TAD KUBLER: I knew Bobby from the band I was in before I joined Lifter Puller. We'd shared a practice space with his band. We had talked to a bunch of different people in New York but we had waited so late before we left on tour that even the drummers we knew had already been asked by somebody else. We were starting to stress about it, and then my friend Dave said, "Have you called Bobby Drake?" And I was like, "God, that's a fucking great idea." I didn't know Bobby well, but anytime I would go to see his bands, it was really to watch him play drums. I didn't even have his number. Dave said, "I think he works at the Amoco station in Bloomington," or something like that.

BOBBY DRAKE (DRUMMER, THE HOLD STEADY): I was working on cars at the time, in Minnesota, and Tad called me up at the shop I worked at.

TAD KUBLER: I had to call information to get the number for the service station that he worked at, and I called up and asked to talk to Bobby. "Bobby, it's Tad!" Bobby's so laid back he didn't even seem that surprised that I was calling. Like, "Oh yeah, man, how's it going?" "Craig and I have this band and our drummer can't do this tour. We need somebody who plays drums. We'd fly you out a week before we left and we could rehearse and I'll send you the tunes, and then we'll fly you home," and he was like, "Yeah, sure." And I was like, "Okay, do you want to make sure you can get off work?" And he was like, "Marge, I'm going on tour." I said, "Okay, I'll email you your ticket. And that was that."

BOBBY DRAKE: I quit my job: "Peace! I'm outta here!" That was my ticket out of there. It was great.

TAD KUBLER: We didn't know he hadn't flown much before and he was—and has been ever since—a nervous flier.

BOBBY DRAKE: Going out to New York was my second time on an airplane.

TAD KUBLER: The plan was that he was going to get in late afternoon, early evening, and we were going to go right to rehearsal. His flight was delayed because of weather in Minneapolis. So I think he sat at the airport for two or three hours, and then got on the plane.

BOBBY DRAKE: I was so nervous. I was going to be late and they were expecting me. So I drank too much on the plane.

TAD KUBLER: By the time he arrived in New York, he was really drunk. We didn't know

Bobby well enough to be able to tell—it wasn't super obvious. He's so crazy all the time. It's hard to know what's drunk and what's just crazy. So we got to the rehearsal space a few hours late.

BOBBY DRAKE: It was a total disaster.

TAD KUBLER: It was a disaster. We couldn't even get through a song. And Craig and Galen were both kind of looking at me like, *Dude, what the fuck is going on? What did you do?* And I was kind of like, *Oh shit.* It was a little bit of a relief when we realized how wasted he was. And so we thought, *Let's call it a night and let's try this fresh tomorrow.*

BOBBY DRAKE: It's funny now, but at the time they were probably pretty worried. It was awful.

TAD KUBLER: The next day, first thing Bobby says is, "So you guys ready to do this, or what?" *Yeah, dude. Sure.* And it went swimmingly. He fit in with everybody really well too. So we did that tour, and then he flew home. We did a couple more tours with Bobby, we did one tour with Judd, and our schedule was kind of getting to a point where we needed something a little more consistent and reliable.

JUDD COUNSELL: I remember having a lot of talks with Craig and Tad, and Tad would ask how we could make it work. But my job wasn't flexible, I had kids and I had bills. We had started to get buzz with *Almost Killed Me* and I'd really had my fill of traveling in a van and sleeping on a floor. When I was in The Hold Steady it was very scrappy. But I had no control—when opportunities were presented, you had to say yes, which made it hard to plan other things. I had other responsibilities. I didn't want to hold them back.

GALEN POLIVKA: He couldn't say to his wife, *I'm gonna be gone for six weeks. I might come back with no money, or I might come back with, like, a couple hundred bucks.* That's just not feasible. So like most grown-ups, he had to bail. I was super bummed out, because we had already put a fair amount of work into it and it was something that people were actually responding to, whereas the band that we had been in didn't really get any attention from anybody. So it's like, *This is actually now getting fun and getting to a place where we play shows that people actually come to. To travel around the country for that would be a blast and I'll have my really good friend with me the whole time.* And so I was bummed out.

TAD KUBLER: So we said to Bobby, "We don't want to tell you to move to New York to join the band. But if you move to New York, you'll have a band to play in." Craig and I sat down to talk to Judd, and before we could say anything, he was kind of like, "You know what? This isn't fair to you guys. You need to find somebody who can do this. And unfortunately, I just can't."

BOBBY DRAKE: When I was eighteen I was touring in a shitty screamo band that no one gave a shit about. Then I thought, *I better get a real job because I'm not going to get anywhere with it.* I stopped pursuing it for a while and became a mechanic—an automotive technician—but I

HOW MANY PEOPLE ARE SHOWING UP IS A PRETTY IMMEDIATE AND EFFECTIVE GAUGE OF WHERE YOU'RE AT

still loved drumming and I wanted to play drums forever. Then Tad called me and here we are now.

CRAIG FINN: *Almost Killed Me* definitely felt good. It wasn't a home run but it was bubbling under. At the end of '04, I remember leaving my company's Christmas party to load in to the studio to start recording *Separation Sunday,* and there was a copy of *Spin* and a copy of *Rolling Stone* that had just come out that day, the year-end issues. And each of them had the ten records you didn't hear but you needed to, and we were on both of those. That seemed like the coolest when I was younger. And all of a sudden we were there. One was even the lead with a drawing of us. And I remember thinking as we were loading in, *Let's make a record that everyone* does *hear.*

TAD KUBLER: When people are coming up and saying, "Hey, I saw you in *Spin*," that's exciting and it feels like you're reaching people, which is what you want to do.

GALEN POLIVKA: What gave us momentum in a totally weird way was the "Pazz and Jop" poll in the *Village Voice*. *Almost Killed Me* was in there. Now we appealed to writerly types. Once that happened, we were on this radar. We kind of knew how polarizing we were, potentially, but being on that list got us on the radar among press people, basically, which is huge. Obviously, rock nerds read the music press and rock nerds go to rock shows. That wasn't a demographic we were aiming for necessarily, but it just happened. And that upped our profile, when people in those circles had to have an opinion about us.

CRAIG FINN: "Pazz and Jop" was a validation. That was the thing about New York. I remember someone saying, "Rob Sheffield was at your show the other night. He thought it was fucking amazing." And I was like, I've seen that guy's name in *Rolling Stone*, but I don't know what he looks like. I remember seeing Kelefa Sanneh write something in the *Times* about an exciting band from Brooklyn. *Uh, that guy was at our show?* So there was stuff like that. The *Spin* and *Rolling*

Stone thing seemed way bigger than "Pazz and Jop." There were a fuckload of rock and roll writers from Minneapolis back then. You had Klosterman, you had Matos, you had Jessica Hopper, and others. There was sort of this weird Minneapolis rock-writer mafia and that was doing a little bit of lifting for us. We had early cheerleaders—Joe Gross down in Austin wrote an early piece. Sanneh, Sheffield, all these people came in. And if there's five journalists in New York from Minneapolis, they knew all the others.

GALEN POLIVKA: It was great. I'm the oldest but not by much, and all of us had been in bands that were unrewarding in that way. I'm sure everybody had fun and did good work, but for whatever reason, things went unrecognized. So it was good to have the enthusiasm that you put into it come back at you. It's validating. *Maybe I do know what I'm doing.* I met so many cool, interesting people doing music, that if The Hold Steady hadn't happened, I still would have found it to be rewarding, but this was rewarding in a different way: when you're actually connecting with people on some kind of emotional level, or there's some kind of transcendence to it. That sounds a little bit much, but you know what I mean. To be a part of something that affects people on that kind of level is really emotional. It's really intense, especially when you've been doing it for small returns before.

TAD KUBLER: *Almost Killed Me* had done okay. But the sort of attention that it got didn't feel that much different than the attention that Lifter Puller had got. So for me, it was still a bittersweet thing. Keep in mind, it wasn't until after *Separation Sunday* had come out that things really started to unfold.

GALEN POLIVKA: It was just a nice encouragement and validation. I guess abstractly, I thought, *Oh, it'll help us sell records.* But our most immediate thing was people at shows. That was our only gauge of where we were and it was the most viscerally obvious: *Okay, we're playing in Santa Fe at a five-hundred-capacity club.* How many people are showing up is a pretty immediate and effective gauge of where you're at. Selling records was already crying over spilled milk.

CRAIG FINN: For *Almost Killed Me,* we were a little belligerent in that our press coverage should show how we were. I think about bands like the Faces—I don't know if Mott the Hoople was like that—and we might have styled ourselves as a Brooklyn version of that, always down at the pub and you can come down and hang out if you like. I will admit some of that was normal and true: I'm a big enough rock fan to know how all that works. I thought that would be a cool way to present it. That was our genuine personality, but also I thought if we make that part of the thing, we don't have to hide it, right?

FOUR

ALWAYS MEET YOUR HEROES

BY ISAAC FITZGERALD

NATE AND I WOKE UP IN HIS CAR. THE SUN WAS RISING OVER THE ocean while nearby seagulls started to fill the morning with their piercing cries. It took me a moment to remember where we were. Santa Cruz. Nate rubbed his eyes and looked over at me. We both laughed, and then winced because of our hangovers. We were down from San Francisco to see The Hold Steady play at the Catalyst Club the night before. The year was 2010. Nate had a car, an extra ticket, and asked me if I wanted to join him, as if I would have said anything other than yes. Staying the night hadn't been part of the plan.

That was the second time I had seen The Hold Steady live. The first time was at the Fillmore in San Francisco two years earlier. They were kicking off their "Rock and Roll Means Well" tour with the Drive-By Truckers, and the place was packed. I was there with friends from the bar I worked at, where I wasted away most of my twenties. The majority of my coworkers were there to see DBT, but I was thrilled to finally see THS. A couple of friends had turned me on to the band a few years prior and I hadn't looked back.

Another one of my coworkers at the bar was pursuing a career as a fledgling music writer. He had seen the set the night before, but had forgotten to take pictures for whatever small music website he was writing for. I promised I would take care of his camera and get him some shots, and in exchange he gave me his press pass. I never did work up the nerve to go backstage, but I did manage to take over seven hundred pictures. Sadly, most of them were of the band's feet—as I did my best to stay at the front of the stage, but began ignoring my photography duties as I got caught up in the joyful elation of loud music and sweaty bodies pushing up against me. It was at that time—and still is—one of my favorite shows that I've ever been to.

Before that night, I was never one for live shows. My teenage years were spent in rural Massachusetts. They don't put venues in the middle of nowhere, and getting from the middle of nowhere to venues proved to be difficult. Besides, who had the money to pay for a ticket? In my twenties I still wasn't going to shows. So I wasn't there in New York City in the early 2000s when The Hold Steady emerged. The first time I even heard a Hold Steady song was in 2005, two years after the band had formed, and I was on an island ten miles off the coast of New Hampshire. Nobody was touring there, either. But I do remember what it felt like, listening to that first Hold Steady song. I

wasn't sure if this music was written specifically for me, but it sure felt that way. It grabbed me and didn't let go.

In those days, I had dreams of becoming an artist, though I rarely shared those dreams with anyone; sometimes I couldn't even look at them directly myself. But the dreams were there. By the time of that first show at the Fillmore in 2008 I was washing dishes in the bar, but every day I wrote in my journal, trying to figure out how to tell my stories the way that Craig Finn did in his songs. Two years later, the same year as that morning in Santa Cruz, I had even managed to publish a piece or two.

Years later, my dreams became a reality. Those first couple of pieces turned into a few more, and eventually turned into a job as an editor. Helping others shape their stories taught me how to shape my own. I even ended up writing an essay about that first concert at the Fillmore, and the story of my friend, the music writer. It was a piece about The Hold Steady, sure, but it was also about friendship and love and death. You know, all those things that you find in a Hold Steady song.

They tell you to never meet your heroes. I'm one of the lucky ones that gets to say: I disagree. The year was 2017. Seven whole years after I found myself waking up bleary-eyed in the passenger seat of my friend Nate's car the morning after a Hold Steady show in Santa Cruz. I had moved back to the East Coast and was living in Brooklyn. The piece was titled "How I Found a Steady Soundtrack for an Unsteady Life." Some THS fans found it and liked it and passed it around on Twitter and in the forums. Imagine my surprise, though, when I saw the name *Franz Nicolay* in my inbox.

Read your piece. I'm in New York. Want to meet for a drink?

That first drink turned into a few, and eventually a friendship with Franz, himself a burgeoning writer, it turned out. Not long after I met up for drinks with Craig as well. This all culminated in me interviewing the band live onstage before one of their now-infamous Brooklyn Bowl nights in 2018. Standing up there onstage with Craig Finn, Tad Kubler, Galen Polivka, Bobby Drake, Steve Selvidge, and Franz Nicolay felt like something out of a dream. A decade earlier I was smashed up in front of the stage, now I was standing on it. I wasn't a music writer. I was barely a writer. Or to be kinder to myself, I hadn't truly accepted that I'd become a writer yet. But pursuing that dream had led to this one. Ten years before, I hadn't gotten the nerve up to use my friend's press pass to go backstage. But that night in 2018 I sat in the green room and drank a beer or three with the band. How often does a boy who never played a musical instrument get to stand onstage at a rock show?

Brooklyn Bowl was packed later that night. I stood in the back of the room—now in my midthirties, no longer as interested in that front row, filled with pumping fists and sweat sliding off brows. Now half the joy of being at a Hold Steady show for me is watching the party itself. The band playing off the audience, the audience crushing up together as they scream back at the band. The magic in the moment. It brought me back to that show in Santa Cruz, eight years earlier. The room hadn't been as crowded as the Fillmore in 2008 nor Brooklyn Bowl in 2018. But even in that half-full room in Santa Cruz, the energy was there. The bodies were fewer, but the magic no less powerful. Any crowd will do.

That night in Santa Cruz, Nate and I thought maybe we would run into the band if we went out afterward. It was such a small town. We hit different bars, looking for The Hold Steady but never finding them. Two bars turned into four, turned into I don't know how many. And then came that

THE
HOLD
STEADY
VOX
Ampeg

next morning, me and Nate waking up in his car in a parking lot out by the beach, not really sure who had talked the other out of not drinking and driving our way back to San Francisco.

It was still early on the California coast. Nate and I decided to head over to the Santa Cruz Diner—the one with the dolphin on the sign—for some breakfast before heading back up Highway 1 to San Francisco. Slowly we began talking about the night before. Swapping stories about what we remembered from the bars, and eventually turning our attention to the concert. Discussing a shared experience, surrounded by so many strangers. What a thing of beauty a live show can be.

The last time I saw The Hold Steady play was again at the Brooklyn Bowl, the following year: 2019. I wasn't onstage that time, I didn't let anyone in the band know I was coming. The room was unsurprisingly packed. I sat toward the back again and watched. The entire spectacle. Hearing Craig Finn sing, "*And we couldn't have even done this if it wasn't for you,*" straight to the audience that he wrote those lyrics for. The magic of live music, something I never appreciated until later in life. Appreciate even more now. That moment right there, because of the band and because of the audience. That's the story of the music—and it's being told in that moment. New stories are getting made right in front of our eyes.

Isaac Fitzgerald is the author of four books, including the memoir Dirtbag, Massachusetts.

FIVE
DOG BITES AND PRODIGAL CHILDREN

FRANZ NICOLAY: They had asked me to play on the release show for *Almost Killed Me*. Once I had played on the recording session, it was almost as if I was already part of the extended universe of the band. That was in May, and then I played another show with them at the Delancey. I did a similar thing, came and played on three or four songs. And eventually Craig and Tad asked me out for a drink and said, "Hey, do you want to join the band?"

TAD KUBLER: He had three or four other bands he was in already, and I said, "It's not going to take up a lot of your time. This is going to be a very low-impact, low-key kind of situation. You'll have plenty of time to do everything else."

FRANZ NICOLAY: I was in a bunch of bands, so what was another band? I didn't think it was going to supplant my main gig. At that point, The Hold Steady was playing Mercury Lounge and World/Inferno was selling out Bowery Ballroom and Warsaw, and their line at that point was, "It's low-key, we're not going to tour," and they were fun guys to be around. I thought maybe I could help juice the music a little bit. It didn't seem like a big commitment.

CRAIG FINN: He's a great performer. He classed it up a little bit. We were all coming on in jeans and T-shirts, and he was coming on in a suit and a hat. Piano wasn't a huge part of indie rock, but it makes a huge difference live when you go down to just a piano break. And then coming back with a big guitar solo is a ride that you can take the audience on. We hadn't had that in our arsenal. It made a huge difference live, both his performance and his playing.

FRANZ NICOLAY: There was a lot of pushback when I first joined the band from people who loved *Almost Killed Me* and were like, "What are they doing with the keyboards?" And I do remember that there were voices when I left the band, saying, "Ah, thank God, he ruined the band, now they can go back to being the guitar band that they were always supposed to be." Those voices have been lost in the dustbin of history, but I'm here to tell you they were there.

CRAIG FINN: A small group of people. Very small. But they were there. There will always be those people.

FRANZ NICOLAY: I didn't have a master plan going in, again because it wasn't clear that it was a big commitment, but I started going to rehearsals and half of *Separation Sunday* was written at that point, but they were still writing. The first one I remember working on was "Chicago," and I came up with that piano bridge. That seemed like a way forward to bringing a broader dynamic range to the songs, just that little four-chord thing, as a piano bridge, a breakdown. And then "Stevie Nix" came later. And then I brought in "Don't Let Me Explode" as sort of like an opening gambit on: are they going to be interested in my bringing in material?

CRAIG FINN: All of a sudden, in the writing process, we're doing things like "Stevie Nix," where we're going down to just piano. And that's a big thing. At the end of Lifter Puller, we were starting to listen to a lot of Bruce Springsteen, and by *Separation Sunday* we had the big, grandiose, "Jungleland" type of song, going down to just the piano. I'd like to say we challenged ourselves, but I think it was more likely, *Wow, this is kind of fun.*

GALEN POLIVKA: Franz added new color and new dimensions. The songwriting got more concise—there's hooks in there. It's definitely a more fully realized thing. We all knew, collectively,

that it was definitely an artistic step up, even while we were doing it. It felt like: *This is actually a thing now*. It was also really fun to make too. *Almost Killed Me* was fun to make, but it was a couple of weekend sessions. *Separation Sunday* wasn't like *Rumours*—we weren't there forever, but I think it's my favorite record of ours.

TAD KUBLER: It definitely felt like there was an evolution happening. That was the first time that the writing started to happen separately, where I would work on music, and Craig would work on lyrics. And then we'd come together and see what we had. Craig has more of a vision for things than I do. Always has. He's much better at stuff like that. I just do what I do, and hope that it fits within the context of whatever we're doing. For me, personally, "Cattle and the Creeping Things" is as good of a song as I'm ever going to write.

Galen and I were actually living together while we made that record. And while we were writing that record was also when Judd was exiting the band, and Bobby was entering the band. So there were a lot of things happening that worked to inspire us. And this was the first record where Franz was actually a member of the band. All those things were super helpful in creating a bigger picture. Or a larger palette.

BOBBY DRAKE: I played on side two.

GALEN POLIVKA: Judd drummed on the first half, Bobby drummed on the second half. Bobby was pretty nervous. Recording for drummers is tough, man. You're waiting for a good track out of the drummer before you can do anything. And with six people staring at you, waiting to get a good take out of you, that's got to be insanely nerve-racking. He was replacing a really good drummer, walking into the situation in New York, and that must have been intimidating. I remember the first day was a little ropey and a little weird and Dave Gardner [coproducer of the album] got him kicking ass and helped his confidence, and he just started nailing stuff. He was nervous. He was clearly like, *Oh shit, these people are counting on me to deliver here.* And obviously, he did.

JUDD COUNSELL: It was fun for me, because at that point I was splitting away from the band. I really loved the Bobby songs and it was fun for me to hear them, but a little strange, because I was so invested in my own part. I really enjoyed making that record, and that really comes across on those songs. *Separation Sunday* was another step in the upward trajectory of the band, which was a bit strange for me because it was my last record. I did have a fear of becoming The Hold Steady's Pete Best and everyone shaking their heads as I walked down the street.

But not only did I love my time in the band, I loved what the band was doing afterward. I was and am very proud of what I got on record with The Hold Steady. And I loved working with those guys as musicians—it was a perfect fit for me musically. It was the music I loved and they were great guys to play it with. When Franz came in, I was like, *I don't know how I'll feel about this,* but I ended up loving that too. It's been as fulfilling a musical experience as I've been involved with.

CRAIG FINN: One of the processes in any Hold Steady record—I'm guessing a lot artists are the same—is the idea of, "Well, we've done that before, so what are we going to do new, what's gonna be the thing?" We'd been together for a little bit. We were playing our instruments more, and we were coming up with more unique stuff. We were discovering some of the possibilities. Maybe we were discovering the parts of the band that people liked, and leaning into those. And yeah, I think the songwriting got better. People had liked the way the last Lifter Puller record had kind of a narrative. I thought there might be something to do there. So it was looking for a way to dial that in.

TAD KUBLER: We were recording it with Dean who we did *Almost Killed Me* with, and with Dave Gardner, who we did a lot of the Lifter Puller stuff with. I'm always trying to get it to sound like a Billy Childish record. Or a cross between a Billy Childish record and REO Speedwagon, which are opposite sides of the spectrum, really.

GALEN POLIVKA: They were party sessions, but it didn't get in the way of the work.

TAD KUBLER: We'd had enough success from *Almost Killed Me* that we were enthused—that would be a safe word to use—and we were partying a lot. It felt like we were coming into our own. Jarvis Cocker has the fucking greatest definition of cocaine: we're inventing the future. That's kind of how we felt. So it was a celebration. And I guess I look at it like that. There was a tremendous amount of partying going on during that record. Because it felt like this could all end tomorrow.

IF YOU PUT THAT MUCH BOOZE INTO PEOPLE WHO ARE HAVING FUN, IT'S GOING TO INVARIABLY GET WEIRD

DEAN BALTULONIS: It was definitely a fun time. But it was after the initial takes: getting the band doing the drums, and stuff like that.

GALEN POLIVKA: Dave Gardner and Dean Baltulonis were a fun team, but taskmasters when they needed to be. In managing personalities, they were great. There was nothing really fraught, there was no real ego-clashing weirdness, or people pouting about stuff not working out, or, "Oh, I'm not loud enough in the mix." There was no preciousness to it, and the material was super together as well. We were really well rehearsed and really on top of our shit at that point. It was a fun record to make. And it was in the city, downtown. Not quite Wall Street, but there's still weird stuff to do around there. And I was super close to my house. So that was easy. There was a night that Tad got bitten by a dog.

BOBBY DRAKE: I got done wrapping my drum takes and Tad was like, "Let's peel out and go to this bar downstairs." At the time he was drinking, and I was trying to keep up with him. He was maybe four, five drinks ahead of me. Whiskey gingers. There was a wild dog that bit him on the ankle. Then we got back and I vomited everywhere. Blue chips. It was disgusting.

GALEN POLIVKA: That was particularly weird, but everything was weird with us then. And if you put that much booze into people who are having fun, it's going to invariably get weird.

DEAN BALTULONIS: I think we spent probably three or four weeks on that record. It wasn't as rushed. We had time to experiment with different instrumentation—it wasn't, "Okay, let's get these sounds quick." We were using different amps for different songs and doing more tailoring per song, instead of just, "Let's get the songs recorded for a demo to get a record deal."

FRANZ NICOLAY: I think there's a split in that record, not just the songs that Judd played on versus the songs that Bobby played on, but the songs on which Dave Gardner took the lead in mixing versus the songs on which Dean Baltulonis took the lead in mixing. Dave has a much wider conception of the sonics of a record. He did those Lifter Puller records that have all those weird things in them and the weird Casio keyboards, and I think he was much more interested in the sonics of the keyboards in the context of The Hold Steady than Dean was.

Dean did, and still does, hardcore records. He didn't work with keyboards; he worked with guitars. He had this concept, which he articulated in the studio, which he called the "rock eagle," which was something to the effect that the mix of a rock song is like a majestic eagle, and the torso of the eagle is the bass and the drums, and the huge wide wings are the guitars, the head is the vocal, and the keyboards and everything else are the feathers. I know Tad loved that concept, and I found it profoundly insulting.

DEAN BALTULONIS: I think my tracks were maybe a little bit more guitar-driven. But I don't really think there was a track that I was like, "Okay, I'm *owning* this one." You know what I mean?

CRAIG FINN: It's a classic prodigal son story—except it's a prodigal daughter—where someone goes away and comes back. Someone can always come back. And that's the beauty of the stories you hear in the Bible. And the ones that are most beautiful are the ones in which someone can come back and be accepted and loved. Once I got into it, I needed to write the story out. There were a couple things I needed to figure out. But let's be honest, it's not a novel. It's impressionistic. So it's some vague sense of where these people went and what happened. That's the beauty and the ease of writing songs rather than being a novelist. You don't have to solve everything to a T. With *Separation Sunday*, there's this general sense of how she goes off with two people and comes back with one. And everyone wonders where she went. That's basically the whole thing.

TAD KUBLER: Even though I wrote probably 90 percent of the music for it, I didn't find out the concept of the record until six months after it came out. But Craig never let the truth get in the way of a good story. Craig always has the bigger picture in mind. So it could have very well been intended as a concept record, but I also think it may have just developed into that.

CRAIG FINN: I had started going to church again, because my wife at the time was sick. I started going to Mass and I found some comfort. I guess I wouldn't have gone if I didn't think I was gonna find some comfort in it. But I found maybe a little more than I expected to, and I started thinking a lot about the role of Catholicism in my own life. I guess I just got a little obsessed, really. I think the Catholicism part of that record was received by people of no faith with greater enthusiasm than by people of faith. A lot of people who had grown up with Catholicism were like, "Ho hum." And I think a lot of people who hadn't were like, "What the fuck?" I mean, there was no place for that in indie rock in 2005. In fact, some people thought it was Christian rock. It wasn't like, "You all should become Catholics." It was more, "This is a heavy thing—people use it to escape, much like they use drugs and alcohol." It was less Christian rock than rock about Christians.

TAD KUBLER: I think it was the first time Craig started becoming comfortable being an artist, which honestly took another ten to fifteen years for him to really settle into. But I think it was the first time it occurred to him that, *Hey, this might be what I do.*

CRAIG FINN: Gideon was a skinhead kind of guy, right? Much like some of the people around the hardcore scene that I grew up with. Charlemagne, I saw him as a classic pimp—not with the feather boa, but whatever the modern version of that is. A tracksuit. Holly was a pretty girl who got lost, maybe someone who had come from a traditional evangelical or Catholic background. I saw her as a pretty girl who was maybe not as connected to a subculture or a real, identifiable, physical scene. Maybe she was somewhat innocent and pulled between these poles, and wanting to

do the right thing still, but she's attracted to the things that those guys were leading her into. The name Charlemagne, honestly, it was ninth-grade history. I just really liked my history teacher, Tim Rosenfield. And he would get so excited talking about Charlemagne, he'd be bouncing on the balls of his feet. I always thought Charlemagne was cool—he's Charles the Great!—and it just sounded like the kind of exotic name someone at City Center might have.

It just sounded right and with a lot of these things, it's about how it comes off your tongue. And Charlemagne sounds like someone we'd be fascinated with. There was a song by the Grifters on the *Eureka* EP—which was influential on Lifter Puller too—that opened, *"Here's the lowdown on the gold boy."* I remember hearing that song and being like, *Holy shit, like, it's the same thing as Springsteen does. Who's the gold boy? What's he doing? And where can I find out more about him?* I wanted Charlemagne to be like that.

TAD KUBLER: *Separation Sunday* exists as this album where we still weren't sure if anybody was ever going to hear it. So we did whatever we wanted to. Which I think is the best way to make a record.

CRAIG FINN: It was not very careerist. I think I didn't allow myself to dare to dream at that point. I realized people liked us, and I wanted to grow the thing. But I don't think in making *Separation Sunday* that I thought it was going to kick off something that would make me unemployable and put us on the road all the time. I thought that there would be maybe 8 to 10 percent growth rather than 200 percent, or however it ended up.

SYD BUTLER: *Almost Killed Me* had such a raw feeling. It captured the initial story of what The Hold Steady would be. But then came *Separation Sunday*. It was a more cohesive record. People felt it was a masterpiece. It was *The Empire Strikes Back* to *Star Wars.* It was the best of the best. The Hold Steady validated Frenchkiss. All of a sudden we had a higher profile and bigger bands would come to us. We sold ten thousand copies of *Separation Sunday*, which was a big deal. My relationship with Craig and Tad is entwined in the success of The Hold Steady. Without the success of The Hold Steady, Frenchkiss Records would not exist.

FRANZ NICOLAY: I remember that one as an emotionally complicated record for me, because that was the point at which Tad and I had to confront what our roles were going to be in the band, and confront that we had different conceptions of what those were going to be. I don't think he had heard my parts, really, in the rehearsal space. I was obviously super aware of them, and so when it came to mixing the record, were they going to be an equal partner with all the guitar tracks or were they going to be these little tinkly bits off in the background? That was the debate, and the fact that there were two producers also made that a little trickier to figure out.

I was coming in, I was twenty-six and cocky about my role in the world in general, but I was thinking of myself as an equal partner in the rhythm section with the guitars, and I know that wasn't Tad's conception of the role that the keyboards were going to play in the band.

GALEN POLIVKA: He and Tad did butt heads, and it never really subsided entirely. Franz is a great musician, obviously. And Craig definitely utilized him in a way that was effective and really smart in hindsight: if you have a person with a totally different sensibility, who plays a totally different instrument, contributing to the writing process, that's huge in how it mixes things up. There's an inherent dislike of repetition in most bands, so just having those two voices in the same band was cute. It spurred healthy-ish competition, you know what I mean? Craig and Tad are pretty type A—they like running shit. And Franz is also a type-A dude, but in the hierarchy of things he was always behind those two. His sensibility was different from Tad's from a songwriting perspective. Or just his overall approach to everything. Which benefited us as a band, but I think Franz felt like he was having his toes stepped on a lot of the time.

But personally, there was very little melodrama. When you play two hundred shows a year, someone's gonna get on your nerves with some consistency for some duration of time at some point. But at the end of the day, we all realized it was just that people were hungover, people were working really hard. We were tired and didn't feel like being super social sometimes. But I think being in our thirties totally helped: "Let's leave so-and-so alone today, or, if so-and-so is being that way, just play the show and the show will be fun." If someone was grumpy or cranky, there wasn't a lot of hand-holding and asking about how you're feeling. Just: "We have a show tonight. If you're hungover, sooner or later you won't be hungover and then you will be in a fine mood and everything's fine."

CRAIG FINN: What had the most impact for *Separation Sunday* was the *Village Voice* piece. When we went to South by Southwest in 2005, we did an interview with Joe Gross. And that South by went very well. I think we were on the cover of one of the daily papers. We kind of crushed South by. When we came back there was talk of the interview with Joe being a cover story. The *Voice* hadn't put a band on the cover in years, a long time. And all of a sudden we're scrambling to do a photo shoot, which we did in LA for some weird reason, and Franz couldn't come. But that was the one that all of a sudden made things go *bang. Pitchfork* may have helped a lot more in the long run, nationally, but the one we felt the impact of was the *Voice*.

TAD KUBLER: A lot of the press was about Craig's storytelling. I think it'd been awhile since people had heard that kind of storytelling in rock and roll. That it seemed like it could only last for so long was a big concern to me more than anything else. I thought, *With this kind of critical attention, the backlash is going to come at some point; it has to.*

CRAIG FINN: There's a *Separation Sunday* promo photo where we're all drinking Bud tall boys. That's a really good iconic image when I think of where we were at. I think two people are high-fiving. And you got to step into the world that we were living in, which was a lot of music and a lot of beers and a lot of inside jokes. It projected that kind of ease that we were living in, that friendship was part of this.

GALEN POLIVKA: It wasn't a forced thing. Speaking for myself, I drank too much, certainly. Maybe it wasn't the most responsible thing to do, but it happened organically, for better or worse. It wasn't like, "During this song we'll bring out a bottle of Jameson." It wasn't this contrived thing, it just happened. It wasn't like, "Oh, this is what rock and roll should be." It becomes part of the cycle of it: have a couple drinks before the show, and then you play the show, and there's drinking involved there, and then you're done. And your brain is peaking at eleven forty-five p.m. You're all wired up. I'm not gonna go home and put on some slippers and read a book and go to bed. That's not how it works. Largely, it was fun drinking and celebratory. But like all things drink-related, it can get dark. And there were definitely weird times. But you're in that bubble of the band, and no one's gonna judge as long as shows are good. You can do whatever you want, for better or worse.

HE USED TO DATE MY SISTER MANY YEARS AGO . . . AND I DID PUNCH HIM IN THE FACE. WE HAVE A BROTHERLY RELATIONSHIP.

CRAIG FINN: There were shows that just bombed, but I'm not sure the audience was always aware of it. There was sort of a tenor to the whole thing that was excited, and sometimes the audience was even drunker than we were. There was a sense of take it or leave it, that this part doesn't really matter. What matters is you all have a good time tonight. Maybe it sounds like he's too drunk, or I'm too drunk, but we're gonna have a good time. And I think the audience largely went along with that.

TAD KUBLER: I was drinking probably close to a liter of whiskey a day. It goes back to the rock and roll lifestyle—you think, *This is what I'm supposed to do.* And after a while, you stop even considering whether or not you want to drink. Partially because you have to. And partially because you just think this is what you do. Do I wish I'd made some better choices? Absolutely. Or some different choices.

CRAIG FINN: There was this feeling that if they're going to take this away from us . . . But there was a moment when I realized they're going to bring that bottle of whiskey every night. It does not matter if I drink it or not, it's going to be there tomorrow. But the first time? "This is free?"

TAD KUBLER: That said, I can only think of one time that interfered with the quality of the show. We'd gotten into Chicago, we got really drunk, I went home with some girl, who gave me some kind of medication. And I was a train wreck the next day. We played early [at Intonation Festival in July 2005], at like one o'clock. And my mom was there, which makes it that much worse. She'd come down to see us and I was yelling at Bobby onstage, fucking pouting and stomping my feet around and all kinds of shit.

CRAIG FINN: Tad was too drunk and was convinced Bobby was playing too fast, which he

wasn't. He was screaming, "Slow down, slow down, slow down!" And that almost ended in a fight that would have broken up the band.

BOBBY DRAKE: There was some weird drug he was on. And he kept turning back to me and shouting, "Slow down! Slow down!" I'm, "Dude, I'm sober back here." It just got really ugly. From onstage to offstage we were separated because I was going to tear his head off. He was a fucking cunt back then. Pardon my language. He was difficult.

TAD KUBLER: Bobby has a great feel. But when it comes to tempo? I don't think that is something he thinks about in the same way that I do. I can start "Multitude of Casualties" seven nights a week and it'll be within one or two BPMs every single night.

GALEN POLIVKA: That's one interpretation of it. Wow. I don't remember what tempo Bobby was playing, but I was two feet away from him and Bobby was going to knock him out. He was gonna knock him out in front of his mother. That was gnarly. It was bad. There's probably shows where I could have played better too, but no one's gonna be perfect all the time, even without the booze.

TAD KUBLER: Bobby has hit me a couple of times. South by Southwest was one of them, in which he duked me out in the hotel room. The guy who was with us was like, "Holy shit! Oh my God!" Galen was like, "Oh, don't worry about it, this happens all the time." But that had more to do with the fact that I dated Bobby's sister years back. And I think he still has some issues about that.

BOBBY DRAKE: The other time, he used to date my sister many years ago. And he did say something about her, wrongfully. And I did punch him in the face. We have a brotherly relationship.

CRAIG FINN: There was one show in Seattle where I got too drunk. That's a legendary one. I was kind of mad at the audience. I was way too drunk, and I threw a microphone into the crowd and hit someone. And I gathered the band the next day and apologized, and reined it in after that, but that one haunts me.

GALEN POLIVKA: Those two shows were pretty much unmitigated disasters. It's disrespectful. It sucks that people got shows that were . . . *subpar* is being very kind. The law of averages, I think, stands in our favor, though. If there's two shows that are total train wrecks, amongst however many we played, I think we punched above our weight.

CRAIG FINN: We were pretty good about talking to fans, but it felt like people were traveling to see us early, for *Almost Killed Me*. You'd be like, "What? You drove *how* long?" But on *Separation Sunday*, you started to see people in the front row every night for a few shows in a row. The cool thing about that kind of touring is that if you're playing six weeks, it's not ten hours between shows—you're playing everywhere. So you're playing Birmingham, then Atlanta, and then Charleston, and so people can do two- or three-hour drives along with you, and see the show the next night. It was around *Separation Sunday* where I really became aware of it.

GALEN POLIVKA: It was weird for me. So having lyrics shouted back at you must be pretty wild, man. It's got to be a headfuck in some way. I can't even imagine. But yeah, we would definitely recognize people. And people would wait for us. They'd be at sound check. We'd load in at three in the afternoon and people would be hanging out at the bar already, kind of wasted. "Yeah, we're going on in about eight hours. Are you going to go home and sleep and come back? How is this gonna work?" People who were into it were *really* into it, for sure.

CRAIG FINN: I was flattered. And a little bit crazy about it. But we had talked about being that kind of band. So in some way, it was like: "Here we are, this is what we talked about, we've

I'VE BEEN CORNERED BY PEOPLE WHO ARE A LITTLE TOO DRUNK AND A LITTLE TOO ENTHUSIASTIC. BUT I'M ALL FOR DRUNKEN ENTHUSIASM.

done it, this is working." I liked bands that you felt a part of. So, while it was flattering, it felt like part of the plan. It felt like part of the design in some way, you know?

GALEN POLIVKA: If some punk rock band was playing in a record store, I was standing three feet away from the dude and could see what pedals he was using and what kind of beer he was drinking. You could smell them—it was like an immersion into everything. And in a lot of cases taking it one step further and going and having a drink with them. I've been cornered by people who are a little too drunk and a little too enthusiastic. But I'm all for drunken enthusiasm. You can't begrudge people for enjoying themselves at your show. That's obnoxious. I'm not gonna blow anybody off or be like, "Oh, man, I'm talking to somebody." They're part of the whole thing. They took the time out of their night to come and see something, and if that involves me being pleasant to them at the end of the night, I'm totally okay with being pleasant.

CRAIG FINN: That was what we took from hardcore. There was a local band, Blind Approach, that I would go to see quite a bit, and they were the best and biggest hardcore band in Minneapolis of my era. And they were like, "Who's this guy up in the front row at every one of our shows?" There were probably only a hundred people at the show. So it was easier, but there was something about punk rock and hardcore that was breaking down the walls. I went to see them so much that they're still my friends. Hardcore gave us the idea that the audience could be a part of it, and the sense of a scene comes from hardcore. And feeling a part of it, feeling a part of something, feeling that the audience and the band are both part of the show.

FRANZ NICOLAY: It was exciting. It was also such a hectic time in my life that I don't think I understood how unusual it was for that to be happening, because it was the second time that something like that had happened to me, to be in a band that was having that rise. Obviously,

The Hold Steady rose farther, but there's a way in which you're in a music scene in your twenties and all your friends are in bands, and you think all their bands are good, and everyone thinks their band is going to do well, and everyone's getting big shows here and there, and you don't necessarily know which bands are going to have the longevity. And so, I think we knew it was a good band, but did I realize it was going to be one of the bands of that generation that was going to have staying power? No.

BOBBY DRAKE: It happened so fast—it sounds corny. We did two hundred and some shows in one year, and that's really busy. Some stuff gets lost in the mix, which is sad, especially if you're partying your ass off. It's hard to be 100 percent cognizant of everything.

TAD KUBLER: We had quite a bit of material. We had the two albums and a few outtakes. And there were a couple of shows where we literally played every single song we knew. Craig had seen Springsteen a bunch at some point during this time, and he thought that was the way to go.

It helped us in some ways, in terms of stamina, but we weren't a very succinct live band: just keep going, like the fucking Energizer Bunny ads. And by the end, because of the amount of drinking onstage, we were a train wreck, which is when the "Killer Parties" thing started to come into play.

CRAIG FINN: On the *Separation Sunday* tour, I thought a good idea would be to play as long as we could. This was the Springsteen fan in me. I thought, *All these indie rock bands are so* *concerned with who sees the end of their set, but why don't we just play all our songs, and people can leave whenever they want?* It was for the people! And that night in Fargo, we played for almost three hours. To sixty people.

GALEN POLIVKA: By the third hour, people were bringing up shots onstage. There was no way it would end well. In theory, it's great, I guess. But I don't want to see that. I don't want to see any band do that. I don't want to see a band get progressively more drunk and more inept over the course of three and a half hours. Why would you voluntarily submit yourself to that?

CRAIG FINN: As I started to push it, you know, I realized that having a good show that people leave wanting a little more might be a better approach. But yeah, it allowed us to fulfill some of the classic rock mythology, because a forty-five-minute set is not what you think of Led Zeppelin doing. Or Springsteen, for sure. And on tour, I was really having a lot of vocal problems, which had as much to do with the goings-on after the show as during, but shaving an hour off each night was very helpful.

GALEN POLIVKA: A great show is one you almost don't think about. This is heavy-handed, but you're looking for some kind of transcendence—fluidity comes up a lot when it's four to six people *so* on the same page that they don't even have to think about it. I think it's something unique in human experience: you're talking to the other musicians, and you're talking to the people with you.

I know this sounds corny, but it's a communal thing, like a spirit or something that you're conjuring with. That sounds really, really mystical, but autopilot sounds like you're punching the clock, and it's the opposite. You're going for that space where you don't have to think and you're communicating everything that you need to communicate. There's something perfect about it, because you're playing with people. Being a bass player is like aiding and abetting, there's a dependability to it that I like. I'm a bed for something and these guys can go wherever they want. Sometimes I'll go with them. And sometimes I won't. And all these decisions, they're not even decisions at that point. It just happens when it's a really good show.

CRAIG FINN: I think it's musical. It's feeling good onstage, but it's the audience getting there too. This is a sort of celebration. Our idea was always to have a celebration onstage and hope that the audience joins in. And so if the audience joins in, that's when it reaches liftoff. When you look out, and you have two guys—and to be honest, it's usually guys—who didn't know each other at the beginning of the show grabbing each other, and singing, and putting their arms around each other, that's achieving liftoff on some level.

TAD KUBLER: The box truck. Oh, dude, I love that vehicle.

BOBBY DRAKE: Oh, the box truck. Where do you want me to start? I believe we got it after playing a First Avenue show, straightaway after that. It was scary.

CRAIG FINN: This is a huge part of the Hold Steady story. We bought this box truck that had been converted by a band in Jersey.

FRANZ NICOLAY: It was the Bouncing Souls. The Bouncing Souls were involved in a business that was converting these box trucks into touring vehicles.

TAD KUBLER: We had been hanging out with the Bouncing Souls guys a lot, and they toured in a box truck. They were like, "Dude, you guys got to do this. This is how you should do it." And so we went out and we bought a box truck.

FRANZ NICOLAY: It was an old refrigerated truck with a big heavy sliding door from the cab into the back, and they had taken a saw to the roof and installed a fan that didn't really give that much ventilation—there weren't any windows. They put in a VCR, a DVD player, and a little ten- or twelve-inch TV. There was a loft bed with a fucking filthy mattress and a sleeping bag and then these two bench seats from vans, from Econoline vans, that weren't bolted down. It was a million degrees in the summer and it was freezing cold in the winter, and you could sort of sleep three guys back there if you needed to, one on each bench and one up in the loft, and then one guy could sleep on the bench in the cab if he needed to. It was pretty gross. I associate it with feeling shitty and hungover mostly, with people peeing in bottles, mostly Craig. Gatorade bottles filled with pee by the door.

CRAIG FINN: Now I think about it and shudder, but at the time it felt great. There was a loft, you could lie down up there; there were seats, there was a TV, there were electrics. And so you'd go in the back of this windowless thing and we'd drive ourselves. It was probably not legal. It was registered personal, but it was a commercial vehicle. And so we kept getting tickets, we'd always get pulled over.

GALEN POLIVKA: It probably wasn't a safe vehicle to travel in, I'd imagine. Incrementally less safe than anything else, but it served its purpose. It got us to two hundred shows a year for a couple of years.

TAD KUBLER: The fact that nobody was ever hurt in that thing is a miracle. Seriously hurt, anyways.

FRANZ NICOLAY: One of the corners had gotten crunched in, because one of the times I drove it, I ran it into some building scaffolding, and Tad and Bobby filled it up with spray foam.

TAD KUBLER: If you're not on a bus, having a mechanic in your band is almost a necessity. And Bobby is a good one.

BOBBY DRAKE: It broke down one time right before we were supposed to go to Boston. We went to pick up Tad, and we shut the van off, and it when we went to start it again, it wouldn't start. I figured out the problem was the van's starter motor. Crawled under there, got it out, replaced it, it fell on my face, gave me a nice shiner. And then away we went to the gig. That was one of many debacles the box truck left us in. Maybe they hired me as the mechanic.

CRAIG FINN: Tad was a great driver. But you wouldn't trust him after the show.

TAD KUBLER: I was always the first one up. Craig will confirm this. When I was drinking, I was always the first one up and ready to go. It was part of my whole "control alcoholism" thing. And then I would do most of the driving during the day—in fact, I would say almost all of it. Then, obviously, the show happens and all bets are off.

My deal was: I'll do all the driving during the day as long as somebody handles it after the show. So wake up, take a shower, get shit together. I'm always the guy that gets a hard time for how much stuff I bring on tour. But anytime anybody needs a fucking nail clipper or a Band-Aid, or some stuff for their hair, who do you think they go to? It's not Bobby. At that point he wasn't wearing underwear and he only had one pair of pants. So drive during the day and get to sound check, take the edge off a little bit. And then proceed on to the show.

FRANZ NICOLAY: Tad did most of the driving, I think because his anxiety wouldn't let anyone else do it unless he was physically incapacitated. We would start every morning usually with the Andrew W.K. record, everybody just dragging themselves into the truck and Tad getting behind the wheel and the opening notes of "Party Hard" rocking us into the next day.

After the show was another concern. Early on that was generally me or Craig. Bobby is the best driver in the band, but drove the least. I think he enjoys it the least.

BOBBY DRAKE: There's drivers and mechanics. That's the rule. I would say Galen is the worst driver. Tad was kind of sketchy, because he'd always try to talk on the phone, and go through an iPod while driving. It was scary. I consider myself a pretty decent driver.

GALEN POLIVKA: We had no crew, and that's what you do. But the fact that we drove a super dangerous van all over the country and set up and tore down everything ourselves and played shows and drank our faces off on top of that, I'm tired even thinking about it. Like, that's fucking crazy. We weren't super young.

FRANZ NICOLAY: I loved the touring. Loved it. The romance of it, seeing the places, doing the thing. But also it made my life a lot simpler when I was doing that, because I was in a dire situation—one of the problems with trying to be in two bands was that I couldn't hold down a job

at home. I was in a pretty dire financial state when I wasn't on the road, and so I was trying to stay on the road as much as possible, because then at least, you have the one thing you're responsible for doing every day, you have free drinks, you can usually get fed, and that was that.

There was a period for about a year where I tried to give up having an apartment—I had gotten evicted, I had moved some of my stuff into the Hold Steady rehearsal space, I wasn't making enough money, and so I said, "Okay, I'm going to be on the road enough, I'm just going to try to crash on people's couches when I'm home," and that was a failed experiment. But being on the road, even under those circumstances, was the most exciting thing and the most reliable thing I had going on in my life.

TAD KUBLER: If you're out for four weeks, it takes about ten days to get sorted out. To get back to normal and everything. And that's even without all the booze and everything like that. When we do the Brooklyn Bowl shows, it takes me two or three days to recover from those and I'm not even getting loaded. Coming back from the *Sep Sunday* tour was hard because I had missed so much with my daughter Murph—her first steps. I missed her first birthday. Those are just some of the sacrifices that you make. Things are happening for you and you might not have that opportunity again.

GALEN POLIVKA: I was tired by the end of that year. But again, we were excited, adrenaline carries you through a lot. The fun part will sustain you through a lot of things and the vibe interpersonally was really good. All of us had been in bands that were marginally successful at best. So when you read about the Troubadour, and then you sell the Troubadour out, you're like, *Wow, we just filled the Troubadour.* It's a tiny room, but those little things make up the whole experience. Even in the moment, you just go, *Wow, I'm really lucky to be here and have these people here.* And maybe it helps with the hangovers, I guess.

CRAIG FINN: It was hard to get through that year without some mental health stuff. There was a lot of adrenaline and I was really excited. There was momentum: not just spiritually but chemically—if you felt bad, you drank more. There was a steady diet of alcohol and that would get you through. You might feel bad all day and you'd have four beers and get onstage and have four more while you're up there and, *Hey, I feel good now.* What was different from Lifter Puller was the sense of momentum. I don't know that Lifter Puller ever sold out a show outside of Minneapolis. Maybe once in New York. All of sudden, in The Hold Steady, we're rolling up to places we've never been before: sold out. And that's thrilling for a bunch of guys who've done a lot of it, but have never experienced that kind of success.

SIX

THE SOUND OF DELUDED FAITH

BY LAURA BARTON

AT SOME POINT OR OTHER, MANY OF US FROM ELSEWHERE FALL in love with America. With the idea of America, perhaps. With all of its gleaming emblems: chrome, Coca-Cola, and prom night; diners and gas stations and Elvis; with the dream of the road, and the West.

We may later fall out of love with America, we may become muddled by its attitudes to health care and gun control, we may find it unhinged and uncontrollable, crying and talking about Jesus. But there will still always be a part of us that remembers America as we first saw it: golden with bar light and beer.

My own early impressions of America were forged by a combination of Bruce Springsteen lyrics and television sitcoms—the bonhomie of *Cheers,* the warm dysfunction of *Roseanne.* There was no glitz. These weren't the glamorous tales of New York or Los Angeles, rather they came from places slightly off and to the side, from what felt like some ill-defined middle, but whose names still conjured a certain romance: Illinois, Boston, New Jersey.

In these stories I found bombast and back talk, a swell of community, characters drawn so keenly, so distinctly, that they seemed to number among one's own kin. But there was a sadness too—a sense of lives derailed, a desperation creeping into the days.

It was some years later when I truly fell in love with America. When I watched it unfurl through the window of a Greyhound bus: a run of highways and IHOPs and Taco Bells, fir trees, and porch stoops, and plains. I fell in love with the enormity of it, and with its strangeness. With all of its darkness and sprawl.

When I first heard the music of The Hold Steady, I found all of those things again. Songs that could blaze with an E Street passion, then turn fragile and forlorn. The sense of disappointment and dislocation that ran through their lyrics, and all of the characters of their scene, the little hoodrats, Holly and Charlemagne and Gideon (and Mary), and the great tangle of their lives.

The songs moved too, but only within their own limited circuit, as if eternally trapped in the revolving doors of some suburban shopping mall. Round and round went their characters, visiting and revisiting the parties, the drinks, the drugs, as if these things, too, formed part of the endless chain-store straggle of America.

Much has been written about The Hold Steady as bar band, of their ability to capture the spirit of genial heartland rockers, their blue-collar preoccupations, the lines that often resurface across their songs, and bring first an air of familiarity, and then the faint sense that perhaps one has once again found oneself sitting at the same barstool in the same bar, listening to the same barfly tell the same stories all over again. It's a sound that suggests we might be anywhere in America. We know which songs the jukebox holds, how the room smells, and how the burger tastes. We know the rhythm of the evening and the temperature of the beer, we know the lights are dim and that at some point someone will do something they regret.

The band set out their stall early—"Positive Jam," the opening track of their first album, *Almost Killed Me*, stalked through recent American history, from the 1920s to the 2000s, from the flappers and the fruits to the sniffling indie kids. Splendor was set up against squalor—beside hippies and the hand-holding, there were soup queues and scabby sores, financial crashes, assassinations, overdoses. There were all of the *"dark parts of large Midwestern cities"* where the songs of The Hold Steady have since bloomed.

I think about "Positive Jam" a lot—how it heralded so many of the songs that followed. The strange queasiness of its shifting perspectives, its thunderous drums, the burrowing guitars. How Craig Finn's final entreaty to "hold steady" sounds like a man disorientated, tripped out on the passage of time.

It's a feeling that runs through The Hold Steady's records. There is often something precarious to their songs—the sense, always, that they could go either way, or turn on a dime: the happy exuberant drunk swinging to barroom brawler. I listen to them with the same sense of peril I often feel when following American politics: *Which way,* I wonder, *is it going to go?*

The songs belong, predominantly, to the Twin Cities, to the home of the Golden Gophers and the drawn-out winters, and the Southtown mall in Bloomington. But there are exceptions: trips out to Pensacola, Florida, for instance, which *"parties hard with poppers, pills, and Pepsi,"* to Modesto and Virginia and Philly, to New Orleans and Maine and on to Ybor City. *"I guess we just needed space,"* Finn notes in "Killer Parties." *"We heard about this place / Called the United States . . ."* Somehow the line seems to carry the ambition of both the European settlers and the hedonistic protagonists of "Chillout Tent," barreling off to a festival in western Massachusetts *"to get messed up on the music."* Both imbued with the sense of possibility before them.

Possibility is a crucial quality in the work of The Hold Steady. For all their beaten-down barflies, stalled lives, dejection, these aren't quite songs of despair. There are always flickers of hope beneath their tales of boys and girls in America having such a sad time together. After all, as Finn sings, it's only some nights, not every night, that he thinks Sal Paradise was right. And there are other nights shot through with fierce, stupid optimism. The night, for instance, that they thought John Berryman could fly.

Even when Finn's words tell of an unassailable Midwestern bleakness—"*We drink and we dry up and we crumble into dust,*" as "Stuck Between Stations" recounts, "*we get wet and we corrode and now we're covered up in rust . . .*"—he is backed by a feeling of musical triumph, flourishing keys, and bright bursts of guitar.

Beneath it all, theirs is the sound of something undiminished, of some deluded faith or spark of hope. It's a spirit that has always seemed to me quite uniquely American—this sense of moving ever onward, upward, this relentless promise. It's an Americanness upon which, it seems to me, all of rock and roll is forged. A desire, despite it all, to stay positive.

Laura Barton is a writer and broadcaster in London. She is the author of the memoir Sad Songs.

SEVEN

BOYS AND GIRLS AND CONFETTI

CRAIG FINN: There was a sense of, "What's next? How do we grow?" John Agnello had come into our lives after *Almost Killed Me*. He saw us at South by and asked to meet with us, and pitched us on making the record that became *Separation Sunday*.

JOHN AGNELLO (PRODUCER, *BOYS AND GIRLS IN AMERICA* AND *STAY POSITIVE*): My wife and I were at South by Southwest and a friend of mine said I had to go see this band, so we went. And we were both blown away. So great. The audience dug them, they were getting a little popular but they were underground. They were great, the characters were great, and I put them on my radar.

CRAIG FINN: We said, "Man, we're not ready to bring in an outsider." Dean, who recorded the first two records, was really part of our inner circle. He lived by us, he hung out at my apartment drinking. I was an adult. We were adults. But we weren't necessarily behaving like it. And John was an accomplished producer. But after *Separation Sunday*, I thought, *Where do we go? We need something to push it up now that people are paying attention.* And so we met with him again. And he was like, "I know how to do this, I've got ideas." And so we started working on the songs with him, which was different.

TAD KUBLER: When Franz came into The Hold Steady, *Separation Sunday* was almost entirely written. So *Boys and Girls in America* is the first time that Franz and I really wrote together. He lived a couple of blocks from me in Williamsburg, and I would get up in the morning and go over to his house and we would spend at least two or three hours just working on music. And it was great. Franz comes from such a different place, musically, than I do. And from almost anybody in the band, honestly. It breathed new life into things. But there wasn't a deliberate feeling that this better be good, or better than the last one.

FRANZ NICOLAY: He came over with an acoustic guitar, I had a little acoustic piano and we worked on a couple songs. I remember specifically working on "Hot Soft Light" that way. Primarily it was him with the initial riff and then me doing some sort of counterpoint to that. *Okay, he's the thesis and I'm going to be the antithesis and then we'll have the synthesis. So whatever he's doing, I'm going to play in the offbeats opposite that riff and that's going to be my main*

starting point for what the piano part is going to be. Question and answer, or statement and counterstatement. That's how a lot of those songs are organized: "Hot Soft Light" is that way, "Stations" is that way, "Chips" is that way. "You Can Make Him Like You" was in the studio at the last minute—I had to record that piano part on two different tracks, because it was so new, I couldn't play both hands at the same time yet.

CRAIG FINN: Songs were pouring out, and we were not putting them through a super-vigorous editing process. In those early days, Bobby and Tad would go down to the space with a case of beer. I don't think they thought they were writing songs, I think they thought they were partying and hanging out. And they'd call me. And then I'd go over there, and they'd been there two hours already. They'd be like, "We got three songs," and they'd play them for me. And I'd be like, "Well, I'll get to work on the words." It was prolific, especially with Tad, who was capturing riffs and turning them into things. And then I was playing catch-up to write the words, because there's a steady supply of things being given to me. I can think of one thing that we didn't turn into a song, and part of that later became "Slapped Actress."

GALEN POLIVKA: Everything wasn't a breeze, and for all my talk of how it all magically fell into place, it didn't always. Some B sides were B sides for a reason. Some aren't as good as others and some of them were a little more arduous or time-consuming than others. But we were three records in so we were better at gauging our strengths and our weaknesses and knew which people would respond to certain kinds of songs in a certain way. We could instinctively know what the other people wanted just by virtue of playing together for as long as we had at that point—it flexes every kind of muscle and you know what works musically. We've definitely had songs that at least a couple of people will go, "Oh, wow, this new one is fucking great." And then we play it in Cleveland, and people are visibly going to get beers. "Okay, maybe we can lose that one." But if you write fifty songs, all fifty aren't gonna be great. There's gonna be a top ten in said fifty.

JOHN AGNELLO: The thing that struck me about the first two records, which I wanted to help them improve on, was Craig's vocal delivery. He has that talky thing, and I wanted to work with him to make choruses with more hooks. At one point, I told him, "Dude, it's not a chorus unless you can put a harmony to it." I was trying to get him to sing more, not just be the shouty guy. At a certain point we could develop songs to make the choruses more hooky so people could sing along.

CRAIG FINN: While John didn't say, "We need a chorus," he would say, "Why don't you repeat this? When the band repeats, why don't you repeat too?" And so we got to playing with the idea of choruses, and wordless choruses. That record really employs those—"Chips Ahoy,"

"Massive Nights." And then there were the singalongs, like "Party Pit." We were becoming aware that if there's 250 or 300 people in the room, if you lead them into something, there's a way to play with that. That was considered on this record. John helped talk us through, and listened to, what we had made, and gave pointers. It was production on that level.

JOHN AGNELLO: There's one song where Craig started riffing on the outro, and I said, "Dude, that should be the chorus melody." Stuff like that would happen: "Dude, you've got something great there—that should be the hook!" I loved pushing Craig because he was great at being pushed.

FRANZ NICOLAY: When we were in the rehearsal space working on "Chips Ahoy," I had been thinking about the classic rock and hardcore pantheon that Craig was interested in and responding to, bands in which the singer didn't have a lot of melodic range or didn't carry a lot of melodic content—how did they deal with that? And so one idea was Lou Reed and the wordless vocal hook in "Walk on the Wild Side"—*"Do, do-do, do-do, Do-de-do, do-di-do-do"*—and then in the hardcore world, the gang vocals. That first Against Me! record had a lot of that sort of thing, so it was like, *Okay, that's another route that we could go down.* And the other advantage of that, of course, is that if you're a band that's still mostly playing for people who have never seen you before, they can sing along to it the first or second time they hear it, in what is otherwise a dense and forbidding wall of lyrics that might be off-putting to people encountering The Hold Steady for the first time. It's an easy toehold to climb that mountain.

JOHN AGNELLO: They had patterns they liked repeating. A lot of songs ended similarly and I tried to help them break out of doing it in too many songs. The other thing on *Boys and Girls* I talked to them about was writing bridges. In the early '90s, I wasn't a huge Oasis fan but I loved the way they wrote songs, so every section could be a chorus. I loved that they had bridges, with hooky verses and choruses. So I tried to talk to The Hold Steady about adding third sections after second choruses. There were a bunch of things we tried to do, but I'm not a my-way-or-the-highway guy, so if they said something I didn't like, I didn't get upset. If I got 50 percent of what I asked for, I was doing great. It wasn't that I was a svengali, but I offered an opinion that wasn't just them in a rehearsal room. I thought out of the box.

FRANZ NICOLAY: There was a little bit of a drama in the studio between me and Tad. The way Agnello dealt with it eventually—even more so on *Stay Positive*—was just to do right and left: main guitar riff is hard left, main piano riff is hard right, and that's the basic sound of the band. I know for a fact that Tad didn't like the mix of *Boys and Girls in America*; he thought the piano was too loud. But, you know, fait accompli.

CRAIG FINN: Frenchkiss was a small operation. They didn't have the staff to support the things we were doing.

IT WASN'T THAT I WAS A SVENGALI, BUT I OFFERED AN OPINION THAT WASN'T JUST THEM IN A REHEARSAL ROOM. I THOUGHT OUT OF THE BOX.

SYD BUTLER: Frenchkiss has contracts for two records. We usually don't ask for more. I was aware of our limited resources. I didn't have the financial means at the time for radio and marketing to support a band like The Hold Steady. As long as they were an active band, we would find success with the two records we had.

CRAIG FINN: A few people had come around and talked to us, and Vagrant was one of them. At first it was like, "Well, I don't know, that's not really like what we think we are." They had a lot of bands with kind of strange haircuts, kind of emo, younger person's music, but they also had Paul Westerberg and they also had Rocket from the Crypt, both things we really liked. And when we met with them, they said a lot of things that made sense to us. One was that they didn't put out a ton of records. And number two, they stuck with things.

Some of the other labels we were talking to, we were talking to artists on those labels, and they were like, "Well, yeah, they throw it at the wall, see what sticks. And if it sticks, they put money behind it." Vagrant had a culture of winning, if that makes sense. Rich Egan, who ran the label, felt like a little bit Southern California jockish to me. But you'd want him on your team, or on your side of a fight or something like that. And I always felt like The Hold Steady was not an indie band in some way. And so going to Vagrant, rather than a traditional indie rock label, made sense to me.

TAD KUBLER: Juan Carrera at the time was our manager, and he was managing Calexico and Spoon and Modest Mouse and all these other indie bands that were doing well. We just wanted to try to break 100,000 records. That was sort of a realistic goal to set.

CRAIG FINN: I wanted it to work. At this point, we were kind of living hand to mouth. We'd had success but there were some things that obviously needed to get done. I guess I was conscious that everyone gets bored if it doesn't keep growing in some way. So it had to keep growing, and I didn't know exactly what that looked like. Maybe it meant going up a room in each town. I wouldn't guess that I knew anything about radio or anything like that. But I think I probably experienced it very much at the level of: Who's showing up? If we were playing for 250 people, what if we went up to 500?

TAD KUBLER: Having a label that was more involved was nice, but I would have conversations with them and I didn't understand what the fuck they were talking about. It didn't have any kind of impact on what we were doing, necessarily. You know, it's like, we're still getting up and driving to the next show, and hopefully it's better than the last.

CRAIG FINN: They didn't try to A&R us. They were really cool. They were like, "We like what you do." I think that's not so surprising. We were in our thirties. My experience was that it was working. If *Boys and Girls* had failed, maybe the second one—if they stuck with us—would have seen more A&R, but I think they were trusting Agnello. And you know, at that point we had a manager—Juan Carrera—who'd come in, just after *Separation Sunday*. Everyone just felt confident we were gonna make the record.

JOHN AGNELLO: We had more time to make and realize the record and make it as good as it can be, but from all my years doing this shit, when me and the band hand over the record, it's the label that helps make it happen. Same thing happened with Kurt Vile when he signed to Matador. They knew what to do with *Smoke Ring for My Halo*. Vagrant knew what to do with *Boys and Girls in America*. It was a whole team effort. I was really happy to be there, but they were great, their manager was great, the publicity was great, the label was great, they hit on all cylinders. They went from van to bus on that record, and it was great.

CRAIG FINN: I got the idea of making it like the inside sleeve of *Kiss Alive II,* which is a joyous photo of confetti raining on a crowd, which I always thought was the most rock and roll thing. We were playing with that kind of imagery already, and Tad has a background in photography. So it was like, "I know how to do this, we'll get our friend Marina, who's a very accomplished rock and roll photographer, we'll get a bunch of confetti, Northsix will give us the room, and we'll go there." But like a lot of things at the time, we were figuring it out as we went.

And I was just blown-out hungover. I got there, but I went to sleep on the stage. There was no one there, we'd put a note on our MySpace page—I think that that was maybe in hindsight super naive on our part. There were a few people, but not enough to make an album cover. And I remember Tad going out and getting a bunch of beer and then going into McCarren Park and

talking people into coming to the club. Meanwhile, I'm still asleep on the stage. They round up enough people, but there still weren't that many people there. But we limited the range of the photo and we had these huge fans.

By this point, I'm awake. We're throwing confetti up and people are in it, and we're just blasting photos. Once we assembled the forty people, it didn't take long. And it cost whatever we spent on Budweiser tall boys. It was money well spent. And that's where the confetti at shows comes from, but really it goes back to *Kiss Alive II.*

CRAIG McQUISTON (TOUR MANAGER, THE HOLD STEADY): I got an email from Tad Kubler saying, *This is Tad from The Hold Steady, and we need a tour manager.* I'd only tour-managed one other band at that point, called You Am I, from Australia. I think there was a US tour for *Boys and Girls in America*, and then a European tour. I said, "Hey, I could probably do the stuff in the States. But I don't know if I have the skill set and I haven't really toured in Europe. So I don't think so." And he was like, "You don't think you could do Europe? Are you intelligent? You'll figure it out—we're all figuring it out. Are you an idiot?" No, I'm not an idiot. And he was like, "Well, let's do it." It was great for me. It was hilarious. They flew me to New York. They said to go to a bar in Greenpoint called the Pencil Factory and they'd meet me there. They were my only real instructions.

So I flew up to New York, I went to the bar, and I had no idea, and we were leaving the next day. The way that the band was touring then, they had the box truck, but the thing was a complete death trap. Tad had rented a fifteen-passenger van, so the plan was for me and their merchandise guy Rustun to drive the van with the merch, and then the band and their sound guy Andy Gustaveson would travel in their box truck, which I thought was a weird arrangement, but it was fine by me. They said, "Well, you're gonna pick up Rustun, and then you guys are gonna drive to New Jersey to pick up all the merch and then drive to the first show."

So I'm in the van and I pull up to the rehearsal space to pick up Rustun. It had been his birthday the night before and he had been drinking all night. He didn't go to sleep. I just see a guy vomiting on the side of the building. And I'm like, *Is this my guy?* He gets into the van with me, and I'm like, *Oh God, here's my riding partner, throwing up on the side of a building at seven in the morning.* That's how the whole thing started.

CRAIG FINN: I actually don't totally remember when I started saying, "So much joy," but I suspect it was on the *Boys and Girls* tour. There was a show at the beginning of the tour, it was in Baltimore. And it was a pretty good show. But I remember it being a little dead, like the audience wasn't quite there. And then Tad, at the end of "Killer Parties," started pulling people up, and it became the stage invasion. And that's something we started doing every night. And people seemed to like that. So "Killer Parties" became this thing. I think that was the first part. Eventually, we backed off on the stage invasions for various reasons. The clubs became too big, things started to go wrong, things became dangerous, things got broken. But that was always a thing where the audience kind of became one with the band.

GALEN POLIVKA: A lot of those things turned into recurring themes. Craig's stage banter happened spontaneously at first, and then he honed it. They just developed over time.

TAD KUBLER: If we were going to be able to do a show in front of a thousand people, it had better be at least the best show they've seen that week, if not that month, if not ever. We were confident that we were able to do that. But I'm speaking for myself: there isn't always that much thought put into it. I do think it's deliberate that we've always tried to make sure people walked away with an experience that had the same kind of impact on them that it did on us. But I don't know that there's a formula for that all the time. So you go up and you do everything you can.

CRAIG FINN: I couldn't pause to think. I probably could have [realized this level of success was not permanent] if I was smarter. Also, when you get out on tour, there's something very simple about it. All you have to do is play the show and pack it up and do it the next day. There's almost a willful putting on of blinders. I thought that we had rejected indie rock or something, and appealed to these forty-year-old guys. I didn't realize, in that time period, a sense of being du jour. I didn't get that we were reaching people who would soon move on to the next thing that was du jour, because I thought we were in some way different from that. It was very much a day-to-day thing. I don't think I knew it was temporary, I think I would have if I had thought it through. It was just: "Let's do the show, and hopefully people like it."

NIGEL ADAMS (COFOUNDER, FULL TIME HOBBY): We had a relationship with Vagrant through the rock side of our labels—we have two labels [in the UK], Hassle and Full Time Hobby. My partner Ian Westley had done a deal with Vagrant two years before The Hold Steady came along, and through that we had released *Crimson* by Alkaline Trio and we'd also worked with Paul Westerberg. Then I'd heard that The Hold Steady had signed to Vagrant and I reached out to them to make sure it would be part of our deal. Quite a few labels were sniffing around.

CRAIG FINN: Full Time Hobby had a deal with Vagrant, and we signed worldwide with Vagrant.

TAD KUBLER: Going to the UK was fucking mind-blowing: to cross an ocean and get to England, which for me has always been the pinnacle. It was everything you could have ever asked for as somebody who wants to be a rock and roller.

GALEN POLIVKA: We knew a couple of the shows had sold out. So that was encouraging, obviously. Most rock and roll people in America are Anglophiles to some extent, so it was exciting. But it felt totally out of nowhere. We were continuously flabbergasted by the amount of interest, and the UK was arguably the pinnacle of that. The response was totally crazy.

NIGEL ADAMS: When they came over, it blew me away, it was so exciting. They were so tight, so direct, and so joyful, which was pretty different to anything around at that time. They weren't fitting into any neat box. Then offstage they were the nicest people you could meet. There was profile [in the US], it was just not a lot had happened over here at all. You could see huge potential for it. For the record label it's the case of joining up the dots and focusing that energy. It's about timing—without the timing and luck, it doesn't always connect. And the band being so good live mattered. You can have a great record and you can have all of the attendant excitement, but they might not cut it and it can really slow the whole process down. And it happened incredibly fast: they were playing the Borderline at the start of the year. By July it was Shepherd's Bush Empire—that was faster than any band I'd ever worked on.

CRAIG FINN: We really went back to the UK a lot. There was a sense that we should strike while the iron was hot. We didn't go for the first two records—apart from one show—so let's see if we can build it. And we were also trying to push into Europe from there. We'd go do a few shows in the UK and then push into Europe, but that never really totally worked. My sense, without really knowing, was that UK fans were more fickle than American fans, and that even if you had a good

THEY WERE SO TIGHT, SO DIRECT, AND SO JOYFUL, WHICH WAS PRETTY DIFFERENT TO ANYTHING AROUND AT THAT TIME

few months or a good tour, it would not last. But what I found when I got there is that the audience was maybe even older, at times.

UK shows start earlier and I always wondered if that helped us—the idea that going onstage at eight thirty p.m. rather than ten p.m. might have helped our cause with some people who actually have jobs. Also, there's a type of man that we met over there, the encyclopedic rock fan, who often also likes Springsteen quite a bit. And that was a type of man that I didn't know about, maybe an *Uncut* or *Mojo* reader. We plugged into something there that seemed to make a difference.

GALEN POLIVKA: Anybody who's been in unsuccessful bands knows the underlying thought is: *We should do whatever is offered to us, because who's to say that anyone's gonna give a shit in a month? Strike while the iron is hot. They want us back? Cool.* The beers are bigger, and the buildings are older, it's fun. My job was just to show up, go to the UK, and drink beer and play shows? Sure.

FRANZ NICOLAY: That was the first time we really felt like rock stars, because the rise had not felt meteoric in the United States. It had been three or four years of really hard touring and playing for not that many people all across the United States. Outside of New York City and Minneapolis and Chicago, the shows were not huge. You can get all the press you want, but if you're in Jackson, Mississippi, playing for three people and there's wild dogs out in the street on a Monday night, and you're getting evicted from your house, it doesn't feel like you're having success. But to arrive in England, and all of a sudden you're in *NME,* you're on *Jools Holland*, the shows are all sold out . . . it wasn't exactly Beatles getting off the plane, but it felt like that.

CRAIG FINN: I liked the people. I liked the early set times, I liked being able to go out after the show. I liked hanging out in the pubs. I liked the short distance between the shows—again, you start to see people every night, the same people every night. It was thrilling to me, as someone who hadn't traveled much, to cross an ocean and have a room of people screaming the lyrics back at me.

TAD KUBLER: Opening for the Stones sounds way cooler than it was. Don't get me wrong: I see pictures of that to this day and I'm like, *Holy shit!* There's 160,000 people, and we're at Slane Castle, where U2 did *The Unforgettable Fire* with Daniel Lanois and Brian Eno. You feel like you have finally successfully embedded yourself in the history books of rock and roll a little bit. And that feels good. You want to leave some kind of mark, you want to be remembered, and it felt like in the UK we were doing things that people were going to recall. I wish there was a more glamorous answer, but we didn't really even see them. It was great to be a part of it and to be able to say that we did it. The experience comes and goes so quickly. Like doing *Jools Holland*—it's over before you really had time to enjoy it. You can just sort of remember that it was great.

CRAIG FINN: Playing with the Stones, that was insane. I saw [THS booking agent] Steve Strange after that at one of the festivals, and I said, "That was really fun, how did that happen?" And he said, "Mick Jagger and Ron Wood saw you on *Jools Holland*, and asked for you." I don't know if that's true or not, but that's what I heard from our agent. We didn't even meet the Stones. But even hearing Mick Jagger onstage saying, "We want to thank The Hold Steady"—wow, that was cool.

CRAIG McQUISTON: The night before, we all went out on the town. I didn't have a credit card or an ATM card that worked in Europe. Whatever euros I had on me, I blew at the bar, thinking somebody would get me home, even though I was the tour manager. All of a sudden everybody was getting up to leave the last bar that we were in and I was like, *Oh shit, I don't have a ride home.* I lost my sense of direction; I knew our hotel was somewhere on the Liffey but I didn't know where. I remember stumbling around Dublin all night because I couldn't get a taxi. I think I got back into the hotel at like four thirty in the morning or something after walking in circles. We had an eight a.m. lobby call and I felt like shit. Then driving out to Slane Castle to open up for the Rolling Stones. We got our gear up on the deck and the Rolling Stones's crew were not very nice. And the Rolling Stones's stage does not have a roof. It was actively raining all over all the gear while we were setting up. Galen tried to watch the Stones from the side of the stage. That didn't go over well.

CRAIG FINN: 2007 and 2008 is a bit of a blur. Most of the band thinks of *Boys and Girls* and *Stay Positive* as being companion pieces. We recorded them in the same studio, with the same producer. And there was a sense—smartly on my part—that if we take a year off college, we're not going back. If we take a year off the road, we're not going back. So let's get another record done. And let's just keep it going. Because this is what we do. We put out records and we tour. We wrote a lot of it on the road, doing that whole 2007 summer festival circuit. You play forty-five minutes a day, sometimes at five p.m., and then you're back at the hotel around nine. "All right, let's go meet in Tad's room and try to write something." So a lot of it was written on the road. We started recording just after New Year's, if I remember, and it came out in July, while we were in the UK. So that was fun.

JOHN AGNELLO: It was evident there were some tensions [during the recording of *Stay Positive*]. I knew things were getting a little touchy and I was concerned there would be issues on the road. It didn't seem insoluble, but they were butting heads. Tad had more of the upper hand and Franz was less of the main guy, and that didn't help. I always said Franz was a crucial part of the DNA of the band. He added so much—the clothes, the drinking stage right, the wacky guy.

TAD KUBLER: At first, it was a relief and it was great to have Franz in the band. There wasn't really trouble in paradise until *Stay Positive*. But *Boys and Girls*, it just felt good to have the sound bigger. To be a five-piece instead of a four-piece. With *Boys and Girls,* we felt we had sort of gotten to the peak—that one and *Stay Positive* in a lot of ways feel like the same album.

WE LIKE THINGS THAT ARE TRUTHFUL, WITH A CERTAIN HONESTY, BUT WE'RE NOT ABOVE SOME KIND OF ARTIFICE

FRANZ NICOLAY: I think *Stay Positive* is the best-sounding record in the catalog. I think it's the biggest-sounding record. I think we weren't fighting for sonic space on that record. We were in a residential studio outside of the city, living together in a big studio that had everything we needed, and John was great at setting a tone of relaxation and creativity, and I don't think any of the songs sound bad! Yeah, I like that record. I wouldn't argue that it's one of our top two or even three records, but I do think sonically it sounds the best.

JOHN AGNELLO: On *Stay Positive* we worked on Cinco de Mayo at Water Music and they rolled in with a blender. The entire day, they're making margaritas. By seven we were doing guitar overdubs and Galen was giving me a back massage. The next day I show up and see all these angry interns with mops—they had gone through so many margs that the floor had to be cleaned. I think the last time I puked from drinking was on one of those records. There was a lot of playfulness.

FRANZ NICOLAY: Everyone hated "One for the Cutters" when it came out. That was a big talking point: "Fucking harpsichord." It was Tad's idea, he was thinking about the Beatles and "In My Life." And I thought, *Okay, that's kind of interesting, let's run with that, there's this creepy Gothic quality to that song anyway.* I have a friend who was a professor at Sarah Lawrence College, just north of the city, who had a harpsichord, so we went up and mic'd it up and recorded it up there. Yeah, I mean, nudging outside the boundaries a little bit, but not that much. It's not like harpsichords are unprecedented in pop music.

JOHN AGNELLO: The hardest thing to do when you're making a record with an artist that's doing great is to make a great but varied follow-up. I grew up listening to Todd Rundgren making every record different. So they were all in for that. We tried different approaches to get different results and we got them. We did so many songs and we had to choose what to put on the record and how to sequence it. Toward the end of mixing I said, "I've got it: let me pick the tracks and sequence them. It'll be great no matter what, and when you guys are on tour and the record comes out, you won't be mad at each other. You can all bond and blame me. This way you guys can just get along." They actually were into it. That's the record where they had "Adderall," but they didn't need another drug song, so I took it off. I just wanted to progress a little.

CRAIG FINN: Rough Trade had come aboard there in the UK.

NIGEL ADAMS: I was desperate to keep them. We did everything to scrape together the money. But at the first show at Hoxton, I remember looking back and seeing Geoff Travis there: *Oh, he's a real music fan coming to see a band he loves.* Down the line, I felt we'd done a great job—we'd achieved everything a label should do and more, and sold loads of records. But I could understand. I imagine the decision was Vagrant's—Rough Trade is a big, long-standing name and they decided to license the next record to them. I was really gutted. I loved working with them. I don't think they did particularly better with Rough Trade than they had with us.

GEOFF TRAVIS (FOUNDER, ROUGH TRADE RECORDS): I had fallen in love with *Boys and Girls in America*. That sparked my interest—it got extraordinary reviews. I didn't know anything about them, and I really loved that. I was at a festival in Norway where they happened to be playing and they were fantastic. I said hello to the two principal characters, and expressed some interest. They were quite an un–Rough Trade band—but what is a Rough Trade band? We like things that are truthful, with a certain honesty, but we're not above some kind of artifice. We like soul music. That's what it is. Anything that moves us and stirs the soul, we are interested in.

CRAIG FINN: I remember Geoff Travis, who we really liked, saying, "Radio's the key to the kingdom here." I remember thinking, *Oh, all right, radio is the way this is gonna get bigger, and this is maybe not a strong point of ours. Could it ever be with my voice, or with the songs we're writing?*

GEOFF TRAVIS: They didn't sound like a radio-friendly band, because their strand of Americana is a lane not many are plowing—they were not BBC Radio 6 Music–friendly and we didn't have much success at radio with them. But then they didn't write a killer single—they came close with "Sequestered in Memphis." I always felt they were close but not quite there. But you get a weird perspective from growing up with *Top of the Pops* in the UK. Jeanette [Lee, co-owner of Rough Trade] and I have old-fashioned views about what makes a good single. We like that Jimi Hendrix recorded singles to make his way in the commercial world, not just albums.

CRAIG FINN: But there was always a feeling that growth was happening. We spent '07 in Europe, but in the summer of '08 when *Stay Positive* came out, I remember playing Pitchfork Fest pretty high up on the bill, and it being massive, feeling massive, and things were growing. Because we ping-ponged back between the US and the UK. We were experiencing different things at different times.

CRAIG McQUISTON: Not very many people get to experience what I got to experience with them, being so close to the band, and taking the ride and shepherding the ride. Usually, when you're hired as a tour manager, a band is at a certain point and they are used to having that position. But I got to start near the bottom with them and take that ride. I've been lucky because lightning struck twice. Through The Hold Steady, I met The War on Drugs, and I got to do the whole thing again. I'm lucky to have been able to take that insane ride with two bands.

CRAIG FINN: You know there are issues sometimes, and you sweep them aside, but you try to address them if they're glaring. It's like a race to get through what you have to do before you start to collapse from the exhaustion and the ego and the attention, to get to a place good enough that you can regroup, rather than just keep pushing forward. Though keep pushing forward might be my personal solution to everything, which doesn't always work.

GALEN POLIVKA: Bands are very delicate ecosystems and some kind of perceived slight can get blown out of proportion quickly. To the detriment of our mental health, we just focused on the shows and the records. We felt an obligation to put on good shows for people, and everything else was secondary, including people's feelings, or where their roles fit, or how many songs they had on a record. It wasn't handled delicately a lot of the time. But I don't think we're unique in that regard, either. We'd got the wind at our back, so let's ask questions later.

FRANZ NICOLAY: We weren't in a great way, in terms of both mental and physical health. What can you say? That's the lifestyle. No one gives you free food but everyone gives you free beer when you're on tour. We had this feeling of momentum, that the machine has to keep rolling, and when you're in the bubble, you can't see outside the bubble. I think we would have benefited from taking a year off, but that was never proposed as an option, and none of us asked for it as an option.

CRAIG FINN: A rock band, in some ways, is a race against time, you know what I mean? I think maybe there was a lack of understanding on that—that if you don't get to a certain level in a certain time, it's not gonna work. Because everyone's gonna get too tired, or too drunk, and drugs and alcohol are gonna get on top of everyone, and everyone's gonna get tired of it. So you really need to get to the point where there's some money, or you're just gonna burn out. And I'm not sure I saw that while I was in it. If I was to manage a band, I would tell them that. At the same time, it was wildly fun.

TAD KUBLER: I think we're terrible communicators, and I think part of it is just being a bunch of guys from the Midwest who are not comfortable talking about how they feel. Franz's wife posted something on Instagram recently. It was part of an article where I was talking about how much I love Franz. And she was just like, "That's why I love these guys. They would never say this to each other. But you put some kind of sounding board where they're talking to millions of people, and all of a sudden they talk about how they're feeling." And she's not wrong. Communication has always been a struggle for us. I don't know that it's necessarily anybody's fault. I think part of it was also the fact that things were happening so quickly, that we felt like we were constantly trying to keep that momentum going. And to keep up with everything that was happening.

CRAIG FINN: There was no sense to me that there was anything catastrophic around the corner. We'd gotten things more streamlined. We'd become more pro. And yeah, we were having fun. It didn't feel like the wheels were coming off the wagon.

EIGHT

THE HOLD STEADY IS FROM LONDON

BY MICHAEL HANN

IT ALWAYS MAKES ME LAUGH WHEN I HEAR CRAIG TALK ABOUT the sensible business practices of The Hold Steady. How they make sure they go only where they want; how they never return to markets too soon. It makes me laugh because for a couple of years it seemed as though whenever I wanted to see The Hold Steady, I just had to leave my house and walk for no more than ten minutes. No surprise, perhaps, if you live in Greenpoint. I don't. I live in Kentish Town, a district in North London.

Koko? Just walk south down Kentish Town Road, then Camden High Street. The Forum? Less than five minutes away, north past the Kentish Town tube station. The Roundhouse? West along Prince of Wales Road, cut left down Crogsland Road. The Electric Ballroom? If I'm going in the stage door, that's halfway to Koko; if I'm going in the front, I have to walk a whole two hundred yards out of my way to approach it from the other side. Yes, feel my pain.

I mean, I've traveled to see them too, and not just within the UK. To Brooklyn Bowl, for those four-night runs. To Terminal 5 in Manhattan for the shows with the Truckers. To Norway, where I agreed to go to a four-day festival for the sole purpose of seeing The Hold Steady. They played ten minutes after I got on site. My main memory of the rest of it is of watching Norwegian metal fans try to set each other on fire while Mastodon played at three in the morning, in the partial light of the Scandinavian summer night. Christ, that was a wretched trip.

To me, The Hold Steady isn't just a New York band; it is a London band too (like the Pogues are a London band). I think of pubs to which I have dragged Craig, which then gained their own small place in Hold Steady lore: of Quinn's, at the southern end of Kentish Town, where we returned for old times' sake in spring 2022, to avail ourselves of the late license; of Tapping the Admiral, my actual regular for the last decade, which noted the sudden March influx of people in T-shirts for one weekend, and put out a sign welcoming Hold Steady fans.

The Hold Steady came into my life at the right time. I needed a band. Not just any band; I needed *the* band. I'd come to music journalism late—I took over editing the *Guardian*'s Friday arts supplement in 2006, after a peripatetic career in magazines and newspapers. I was already a fan—I was in my midthirties, of course I was a fan—based on buying the first two albums off iTunes after reading *Pitchfork*'s reviews. But The Hold Steady was just an American thing. They never came to the UK (I didn't know there had been, bizarrely, one UK show, opening for Les Savy Fav in 2005); their records weren't available here. No point them being the band I was going to cheerlead for if they weren't going to take any notice of the UK.

Then, in the autumn of 2006, an email from a publicist, announcing the first UK release by The Hold Steady. I wrote straight back: *THANK GOD SOMEONE HAS FINALLY PICKED UP THIS BAND FOR THE UK*. I interviewed Craig for a little puff piece. I reviewed *Boys and Girls*, gave it five stars. And when they came over for what everyone now counts as the first UK show, I was there. Now, bear in mind, I had never seen an actual clip of The Hold Steady at this point—it's early 2007, and YouTube is still in its infancy. The big thing everyone is talking about is whether the

YouTube clip of the Velvet Underground playing "Sister Ray" on *The Lawrence Welk Show* is real or faked (faked)—so all I knew was what they looked like. I didn't know what they were actually like. I didn't realize they weren't like other bands. No one stared at the floor. Not once. And no one in the crowd took their eyes off the stage.

I left the venue afterward, and the publicist texted me to see if I wanted to come back to meet Craig. I usually say no to those invitations: who the fuck wants to have a stranger foisted on them after playing a ninety-minute rock and roll show, and why the fuck do I want to talk to someone who doesn't want me there? I don't know why I said yes; given that for all he looked mild-mannered, Craig's writing suggested he was an agent of chaos, and I do not like agents of chaos. But I'm glad I did, because without that meeting a whole lot of the subsequent decade and a half would have been very different for me. I remember only that we talked about sports and the Modern Lovers. And then I remember that suddenly there was no one else in the bar, all the other chairs were on tables, and it was three hours later. Craig pulled out his hotel key card. "Do you know where my hotel is?" He was in luck: it was on my cab ride home. And from then on, more or less, we were friends.

I was surprised the UK took to The Hold Steady in such numbers and with such fervor. In London, they went from a 250-cap room to a 2,000-cap room in six months. And along the way they picked up people, like Pied Pipers with electric guitars. People began to follow them. We started nodding to each other at shows. And in some cases rather more than nodding.

Do you know Howard Roberts? If you don't, he's a lawyer based in Yorkshire, in northern England. But since you're reading this book, there's a good chance you know his name at the very least. (I was once asked if I was Howard at a Hold Steady show in New York, just because I have an English accent. When I said I wasn't, the reply was, "You must be the other one." Turns out I wasn't the other one, either.) You've probably heard his name spoken from the stage. You've very likely been bought a drink by Howard. Howard has come to embody the legend of The Hold Steady. Legend, rather than reality, since The Hold Steady no longer spend shows drinking like they're at a Hold Steady show, but Howard does. It was Howard who gave his credit card to the young man—another English guy—who was about to fly to the US to sell merch for The Hold Steady on a US tour. ("This is the first time being a loyal fan of The Hold Steady has translated into financial recklessness," Craig observed.) It was Howard who was once photographed buying a round of forty-six beers at the Bush Hall in West London. (I know it was forty-six. My friend who had not yet met him took a photo of him at the bar, and we counted the beers. "Oh, that's Howard," I said, as if that explained everything.) Howard got himself season tickets for the fucking Minnesota Vikings because he loved The Hold Steady so much. That's a long, long trip to watch a sport in the freezing cold where you can't even see the ball.

I'd say that was bonkers behavior. But what I love about The Hold Steady is how fans feel they have been given permission to do things they might not otherwise do. And that need not necessarily involve alcohol, controlled substances, and risk to either health or liberty, though sometimes, undoubtedly, it does.

At fifty-two years old, I had a black sheep tattooed on my right forearm, a detail from the cover of *Out of Step* by Minor Threat. Minor Threat is not my favorite band; "Out of Step" is not my favorite song of theirs. I am not straight edge and never have been (admittedly, I was neither having sex nor taking drugs when I first heard them, as a teenager, but that wasn't through choice), and I'm no one's idea of a hardcore scenester. But I loved the notion of their personal liberation through rock and roll, even if theirs was the most high-minded and self-denying self-liberation you could imagine. I love so many artists who have used rock and roll to try to find truths about themselves—

Jonathan Richman for one, Ezra Furman for another (and how I cheered when Ezra opened for The Hold Steady at Brooklyn Bowl). The Hold Steady did that for me.

That sheep on my arm isn't about Minor Threat or *Out of Step*. It's about how rock and roll enables me to find something in myself that isn't there when I'm being a dad or doing the shopping or trying to get the parking permit sorted. And the band that let me be myself was The Hold Steady. Honestly, the notion even ten years ago that I would have gone to Brooklyn on my own to watch a band for four consecutive nights would have been ridiculous; the idea that it might become my favorite four nights of the year would have been incomprehensible. I do not talk to strangers in bars. Well, I didn't. Until I started going to the Massive Nights shows. (And what do you know, here's the woman who's an Olympic weightlifter who's flown across the Atlantic for the shows too. You meet all sorts after a Hold Steady show.) I do not get involved in putting my own money at risk for rock music—oh, now I do, because Craig's emailed to say he's got a spare night on a UK tour, and do I reckon Laura Barton and I can put on a show? Damn right we can, and we will make this show unlike any other. (And we did; in front of one hundred people in a faded seaside resort. All shows should have a raffle between the main set and the encore, if you ask me.) The Hold Steady didn't almost kill me; they brought me to life.

When I look around at a Hold Steady show, I see people like me. I don't mean white, middle-aged men, though I see a lot of them. I see people who had needed a band to invest in, to reconnect them with a feeling they had when they were fifteen or sixteen or seventeen and thought they had lost forever, and The Hold Steady was that band for them. For us. And I think in the UK that feeling can be particularly acute, because they represent an Americanness that a lot of us dream of—approachable and ordinary, but with a kind of wildness that is baked into American culture in a way it's not in the UK. Yes, Britishers take as many drugs and drink as much booze as Americans, but there's nothing untamed about Britain. No one in the UK ever turned to someone else and said, "Let's just drive. Let's just hit the road and not stop. Not until we get to . . . Wolverhampton," put it that way. I think if you're British, The Hold Steady represents something so quintessentially American that it might be hard for actual Americans to understand.

The Hold Steady means something different to me now than fifteen years or so ago. Back then, there was the sense that one was riding a wave—here was a band on the up, and seizing their chance with so much gusto one worried about their long-term prospects for survival.

August 2008, at the Rescue Rooms in Nottingham (I've persuaded my wife to combine a visit to her parents, who live nearby, with Friday night at a rock and roll show), and Tad decides he wants to—no, needs to—climb the staircase at the side of the stage. But rather than solo in triumph from the balcony, he decides his solo should be played while sliding down the handrail. At the bottom he flies face-forward onto the stage and lands on his hand. Craig tells me later he fractured his wrist. (I

don't care if he didn't; print the legend.) That was halfway through the show. The show didn't stop.

I remember the stage invasions, the band reaching the end of each set looking like they had just spent the weekend at Altamont. (In fact, when I look at footage of The Hold Steady from 2007, I am struck by how ill they look, always. Like the only green thing they have seen in weeks is the glass of beer bottles.) I remember Craig and Tad coming into the *Guardian* to record a podcast with me, and both asking if I could perhaps spare some aspirin or other painkiller. (I'd been to the pub with Craig the night before. While I'd gone home to bed, he'd gone to sit in the lobby of the Jury's Inn on Pentonville Road, drinking takeout beer with the rest of the band, until the concierge explained to them that the people who were staying there on business would be getting up soon, and it wasn't a good look for the hotel to have five very drunk Americans sprawled around the lobby surrounded by empty cans.) I think of taking Craig to watch cricket at Lord's that first summer they were here and his big takeaway being: "They let you bring in your own beer? Awesome!" I remember every show feeling like a first night, and we did the "Been Caught Stealing" into "Dancing on the Ceiling."

These days the band aren't drunk. Nor am I, usually (unless Howard's going to the bar, in which case I am very, very drunk). These days the band is playing, and I'm listening. I'm listening to the way Steve's and Tad's guitars intertwine like vines on a trellis, and how their embellishments

make the songs bloom in different places. I'm listening to Galen and Bobby, the rare rhythm section in rock and roll that can both swing and bludgeon, and the way they make the songs hurry along. I'm listening to Franz taking things off in another direction entirely, and to Craig spitting out the words, waiting for the line he'll forget. There's always one line. Always.

But some things don't change. What lies beneath remains the same. I've seen this band more times than I can possibly count. I have listened to them more than any other band. And every time I feel the same. "*She said, 'Always remember never to trust me' / Ahhh, she said that the first night that she met me.*" Fuck, this is great, "*She said, 'There's going to come a time when I'm gonna have to go with whoever's going to get me the highest.*'" That's why I still go to The Hold Steady. They get me the highest.

Michael Hann is a writer based in London. He is the author of Denim and Leather: The Rise and Fall of the New Wave of British Heavy Metal.

THE

NINE

THE ER AND THE AFTERBAR

CRAIG FINN: The wheels came off the wagon when Tad was forced to stop drinking. I think it probably could have rolled a little way farther. That's my take now.

TAD KUBLER: *Stay Positive* came out. We did a short run of US dates. And then we did a short UK run. We got home, we were supposed to be home for a couple of weeks, and then go back and do six weeks in the UK and Europe. When we got back, we shot a video for "Stay Positive." And it was that evening when I knew something's not right. Like, I don't feel well, and I'm not somebody who gets sick that way very often. The next morning I woke up and I thought I had kidney stones, or something like that. A couple of days went by and it got progressively worse. And I finally called my doctor at home and I was like, "I am in an insane amount of pain." Knowing me and knowing what my lifestyle was, he said, "Go to the hospital. Go right now. I will be there in the morning."

He told me to go to Beth Israel, which was on the East Side. I was living in Manhattan and I was living on the West Side Highway, just below 14th Street. I made it to Sixth Avenue in a cab before I got out and started throwing up. Luckily we were right in front of St. Vincent's Hospital. I went in there and they did some tests. It was a Friday night and it was so busy. I'm thinking, *Nothing good is happening here.* Anyways, they finally got me on some medication, morphine or whatever, and they got me into intensive care.

CRAIG FINN: I was hanging out having a last dinner before I went on this big tour. The phone rang and it was our tour manager, McQ, and he said, "Have you heard?" And I said, "Heard what?" "Tad's in the hospital." It was pancreatitis, and I think I knew we were not going to be making the first show, or getting on the plane. What developed after that, things were pretty bad: we're going to postpone the tour. That decision was made pretty quick, once we realized he was pretty sick. By the time we went to visit him, he was in bad shape and it looked like he was going to be staying for a while.

BOBBY DRAKE: It was frightening. When that happened, it took a lot of gas out of the tank. Uncertainty everywhere.

FRANZ NICOLAY: I don't know if any of us took that as much of a warning sign as maybe we should have. I think it was more like, *Ugh, sucks for him.* But he was always the one in the band who prided himself on taking it farther and harder than anybody else, so it wasn't exactly a shock.

GALEN POLIVKA: Seeing somebody in the ICU is intense. It was scary. It was kind of melodramatic. It wasn't like, "Oh, he has the sniffles." For Tad to bow out on a tour, he had to be incapacitated. He was in rough shape.

CRAIG FINN: There was a tube down his throat and when they took it out, it hit one of his teeth and broke it. So not only was he in the hospital, but he had this rough-looking tooth up front. I think it was probably more serious than I thought. I think if you're staying in the hospital for ten to fourteen days, there's some chance it could have gone a lot worse.

TAD KUBLER: I was in intensive care for the next five or six days and I was pretty out of it. I don't think I totally understood what was happening. And then once I was out of intensive care, my brother Toby told me that my mom had called him and said, "If you're going to come out, you better do it now, because they don't know if he's going to get better." Which just fucking blows my mind. Listen, I drank a lot. But there are a lot of people who drink more than I did. But my dad's got high blood sugar, my brother has diabetes, so it makes sense that when something finally went wrong, it was related to insulin and how my body breaks down sugar. So that happened. I remember so little of that time period. I do remember, once I was out of the ICU, Craig being there a lot. I would wake up and he would be sitting in my room reading the paper. I guess everybody thought I was gonna die. So, yeah, that was intense.

CRAIG McQUISTON: That would have been really the key European tour for The Hold Steady. They never recovered from that. They still had a great following in the UK, but that was going to be a huge tour for them. I think that was October. So as a crew person, you just lost all of your work for the fall. Monetarily, it was devastating for anybody who worked for the band. And it was devastating for the band.

CRAIG FINN: It was a huge blow and I think later I realized how big of a blow it was. Because from a business standpoint, we were coming off those festivals in places like Sweden, Holland, and Belgium that had gone very well. And now we were following up with our first real club shows, which could have set up a better trajectory in mainland Europe. When we rescheduled that tour, we just went back to the UK. So we never really made up those shows we were supposed to.

GEOFF TRAVIS: It didn't help. The essence of The Hold Steady is building a ground base from playing live, and if that doesn't happen, it makes it harder. But illness is illness.

GALEN POLIVKA: We all could have slowed down a bit, you know what I mean? Did his lifestyle contribute to it? Sure it did. But it could have been any one of us really. In terms of self-abuse or whatever you want to call it, we were all in a weird place. Me scolding Tad with a whiskey in my hand at midnight probably wouldn't have gone over too well. I wasn't any kind of pillar of moderation, by any stretch of the imagination. There's just this bubble where you exist, and as long as the shows are okay and everybody's getting along reasonably well, no one's here to tell anybody what to do. It was just how we operated. These things creep up on you and come out of nowhere, and it was terrifying.

CRAIG McQUISTON: We thought, *Okay, well, he'll get it together.* And then slowly he fell into other things.

TAD KUBLER: I was on a lot of medication when I left the hospital. And then I got into drugs. Here's the big thing for me: I'm in a band that is now successful, and we have carved out this place for ourselves and what we do, and part of what we do is party. And now I can't party anymore, so what the fuck do I do? People are telling me that I can't be a part of this anymore, that I can't participate in this the way everybody else does. And I'd never been onstage sober to this point, ever. It was really scary that way. *They told me I almost died? Yeah, that's kind of scary, but people are telling me I can't do what I do.* That's the way you start to look at it. Now I don't know what to do anymore. Because I can't be who these people are telling me I ought to be. And it took me a long time to figure that out. I wish I would have figured it out a lot sooner.

Unfortunately, for me to evolve, or for me to change, there needs to be some kind of external force. Whether it's becoming a father, whether it's getting pancreatitis and being told that I can't do this anymore, there needs to be an external force. And it usually needs to be significant. If I'm gonna look back on my life and see where I grew, or where things started to change, there's always been something like that.

GALEN POLIVKA: I'm not saying my behavior changed all that much, but we had to show consideration. Approaching something without booze that he was so used to approaching with booze was a huge adjustment for him. I think he had a struggle, thinking, *Wow, can I do this without booze?* There's a ritual around shows: in mine and Tad's, booze was certainly a pretty big part of the equation. So to have that out of the equation overnight, it's got to be nerve-racking. We tried to be on better behavior just out of consideration to him, to just make it more of a comfortable environment for him, because we had to meet him somewhere. He was approaching things in a completely different way, not by choice. Everybody was conscious of that adjustment and tried to compensate to make it more normal for him.

I'M GRATEFUL THAT EVERYBODY WAS ABLE TO STICK IT OUT, BECAUSE IT WASN'T EASY. I WAS A MISERABLE PRICK.

TAD KUBLER: It took me two or three years to even get comfortable onstage playing. I can't believe I played as many shows as I did that loaded. The adjustment took a long time, and I'm grateful that everybody was able to stick it out, because it wasn't easy. I was a miserable prick.

FRANZ NICOLAY: It changed the live show, for him to be sober. And that sort of balls-to-the-wall energy of him both as a songwriter and as a performer—it's a complicated and ambivalent thing to talk about, because thank God he's healthy and sober—I think that's part of the live show that we're never going to see again. I had my issues with Tad as the logistical leader of the band; but Tad as the spiritual leader of the band was really important: Tad as the party starter, Tad as the guy who brought that anarchic energy, on- and offstage, is something that's specific to those years. There's a satisfaction in the professionalism that we have now, but very few unexpected things happen these days.

CRAIG FINN: Tad, when he was drinking, was leading us into battle. He was procuring the booze if there wasn't any—it was part of his thing. He was in no way a bad drunk or anything; he was pleasant. But he was really leading the charge. That went away when he stopped. I never remember thinking Tad should stop drinking. It was that he *had* to stop drinking. There was a loss of looseness onstage, at least for a while. And I guess we all realized it's not going to go very well if we all just keep carrying on the exact same way and he doesn't, so maybe we should try to get a little more pro and try to make this like a big rock machine. And that's where we tried to go.

TAD KUBLER: I felt there had to be something [to replace alcohol], and drugs were something that was mine. Nobody in the band was gonna follow me down, thankfully. It was a way for me to disappear a little bit. There's resentment and stuff that goes into that. There's a lot of different things. I realize how absurd this sounds, but it was the natural progression of that disease or whatever you want to call it. *All right, I can't drink anymore, so I guess I'm going to go pro*. And it became a good way for me to retreat. There's that meme of Homer Simpson disappearing into a bush, and that's kind of how it was. It's difficult to talk about because there isn't anything that's going to sound reasonable.

GALEN POLIVKA: I'm not saying that I'm unfamiliar with drugs. But whatever's going on with him is his business. After he turned sober, we didn't really hang out that much. For a newly sober person, especially at that time, I probably would not be everybody's first choice of companion. I didn't know what was going on, because we didn't really communicate. We were in different places in terms of, well, everything. When we were both drinking, he was crazy and unmanageable, in a way that was not that crazy and kind of manageable. *Oh, he's just loaded*. I didn't feel like it was on me to say anything. Any kind of judgment coming from me, I thought would be inappropriate. And everyone had enough of their own stuff. Everyone was battling something.

CRAIG FINN: So 2008 was the hospitalization, and then the Truckers tour happened, which I think of as a high point in some way—that was a band that influenced us, and suddenly we're coheadlining with them and driving around the country. And it was really fun. But when you talk about tension, I think there was tension between Tad and Franz. I think Franz was probably bringing in songs that we weren't pursuing. And when we were pursuing something like "Yeah Sapphire," sometimes it felt like Tad was a little threatened by it. We had dragged Franz into the band, and I think Franz started thinking, *Well, I'm writing songs that no one's playing, I'm writing songs on my own. I might as well just try to do something else and give it a shot. And now's the time.* That was part of it too: we'd had four critically acclaimed albums. The next one, just by the law of averages . . .

GALEN POLIVKA: Franz certainly has opinions, and he was contributing to songwriting. What starts as a healthy competition can get weird, you know what I mean? The standard rock-biography line is that you need those foils, butting heads. But that has to give at some point. When some people's expectations aren't met on their role in the band, they get frustrated. I can't speak for Franz, but for whatever reason we gravitated artistically more toward what Tad does than what he does. He had aspirations to write his own songs and perform them and tour them under his own name. And our schedule wasn't really all that forgiving in that regard. There's a lot of factors in there. Personality-wise, they're different, but it never manifested itself in fisticuffs or melodrama. It was just two guys who were trying to establish some kind of roles. It wasn't that divisive—it was just, *I hope they sort that out.*

FRANZ NICOLAY: I got the distinct impression that Tad wanted to reassert musical control over the band after *Boys and Girls* and *Stay Positive*. He wanted to produce the next record. It was going to technically be Dean, but Tad was really going to produce. Everyone's seen *Get Back,* and whether you think George Harrison's being an asshole or not, or being a little baby about his role in the band, that is more or less how I was feeling at that point: *I'm in a band with two guys who have a long history and a long creative partnership. I'm creating a lot of music, there's no place for it in this band, and I need an outlet for that.* I had put out this solo record and I was touring it around a little bit; I had heard from Juan—not from Craig or Tad directly—that they were annoyed that I had this other thing going on. It felt like these guys want 100 percent of my time, but also it doesn't seem like they want me to be contributing creatively, and in fact, it seems like Tad wants to turn back the dial on that.

The other thing was, I was still in financial trouble. We still weren't making much money in the band, and the finances of the band were a real black box. I've used this analogy before, but if you're the ambitious young lawyer in the law firm and you can tell you're not going to make partner—ever—you're going to leave and start your own firm. And also, do I trust these guys with the future of my career and life? And Tad was not in a good way at that point and he was super unreliable, and I didn't know if I trusted this guy. All that stuff seemed like it was coming to a head, and I had to either commit myself 100 percent to this band where I was going to be writing B sides for the rest of my life, and I didn't have a lot of faith in—specifically in Tad's reliability going forward—or I could stake out my own territory, and this would seem to be the moment.

TAD KUBLER: Franz came into this very guitar-heavy band. It was a rock and roll band, which is not something I think he was totally comfortable with. He really wanted to plant his flag, and I did not really have the skill set to adequately communicate: "Hey, you're a really important part of what happens here, but this is our thing and this is what we do, and we want you to be a part of this—what can we do to make this so you're not unhappy?" All it takes is one person that's miserable in a band, and then everybody's miserable. I don't understand why there aren't more reality shows about rock bands. Because just from an anthropological standpoint, or a sociological standpoint, they're all a little bit different, but they're impossible relationships. It isn't very often that there's a band where everybody's comfortable with their role, and doesn't want something different.

I think that's what started to happen around *Stay Positive*. And by not talking about it, and not really dealing with it, and hoping that it would just work itself out or get better, it eventually just started to fall apart. I also think we should have taken some time off. Because of my relationship with Steve, when he came into the band, I really made the room for him that I should have made for Franz. I wish I would have done a lot of things. I wish I would have had one less drink every night too, but I had a lot of growing up to do, and I didn't really get a chance to do that until we were able to take a break.

FRANZ NICOLAY: Always in my head at that time was my experience with World/Inferno versus my experience with The Hold Steady, and one was like, *These are my best friends that I'm going drinking with, we're hanging out before and after rehearsal and nights off,* and I didn't have that relationship with the Hold Steady guys. We were just . . . much more so at that point than now, we were just different types of people. I was the only one who wasn't a Midwestern guy and I was the guy who valued dressing up. Their whole presentation was about being as normal as possible, and mine was about being this collection of affectations, which I think had some benefit onstage: I was like the Flavor Flav. You know, they talk about putting one drop of really terrible smell in a perfume to make the whole thing bloom: the weird thing that doesn't fit and makes the whole thing work.

CRAIG FINN: I don't know if I didn't understand it, or if I was cocky. I just remember being like, *Well, it is what it is*. I don't know if that was a defense mechanism. I'm not sure. I don't really

remember. But I remember not being as troubled by it as I think, with hindsight, I should have been.

TAD KUBLER: I felt like I was at the end of my rope with Franz, but I was so used to being unhappy that that could have gone on for another decade. Franz left—like, it wasn't a thing where he was kicked out or anything. I just think the bad vibes got to a point that were intolerable for everybody. But when he actually left, I was freaked out. I was concerned about what it would mean for the band in terms of optics, and what it would mean for the band musically. I guess trying to shoulder maybe the lion's share of the creative side—or at least the initial inspiration part of it—was pretty scary.

GALEN POLIVKA: *Heaven Is Whenever* has moments. There are things on there that I like. Not to bring it back to Tad, but in the middle of that session, he got sick again. Dusty, our guitar tech, who was up there during the recording, drove him off to a hospital. Me and Bobby Drake, there was some kind of lounge, and we just sat side by side and watched the entire *Star Wars* trilogy and probably didn't say a word. We sat there in shell shock, just thinking, *Wow, I hope he survives it.* It was ropey, man, I don't think anyone really knew what to do.

CRAIG FINN: There was the sense the album needed to be big—we needed to have some choruses, we needed to be on the radio. The label was saying a few things, but they weren't harping on it. It was just mild suggestions: "It would be good if you guys had a song for the radio this time." Which I wasn't obsessing over, but I think it got to me a little. Certainly, with song

A LOT OF THAT RECORD HAS THIS WEIRD ADVICE TONE. I DON'T THINK I WAS IN A PLACE TO BE GIVING ANYONE ADVICE.

structures, I started to think, *What's the chorus? Let's have a big chorus here*. Which isn't really our strong point.

BOBBY DRAKE: It was the hardest record I've ever made. Let me tell you, I was doing everything, kicking tons of ass. And Koob would turn up and fucking fall asleep at twelve o'clock. On drugs. And it went on for far too long. And everyone seemed to check out, not knowing what the hell was going on. We were kinda rudderless.

DEAN BALTULONIS: Tad definitely was not in a good way. *Separation Sunday* is one of my favorite records that I recorded. And I think *Heaven Is Whenever*, as far as the experience in the studio, is probably one of my least favorites. It was definitely a tough one. There was definitely tension, but it was kind of underlying. They had been touring together a lot. There was tension from being on the road so much. And they jumped right into doing a record they were trying to write in the studio. Whatever tensions they had just got put under this microscope.

CRAIG FINN: I think we could have tried to do it ourselves. We were struggling to get Tad to be in the studio at the same time we were. He was kind of always trying to engineer it so he came in later and worked on stuff just with Dean. We were not ready, especially given our communication problems, to do it without a strong producer. Dean Baltulonis is a great producer in his own right, but he'd become such good friends with us that he had no authority.

DEAN BALTULONIS: On a record like that, you just get from one end to the other, separating people and working on one thing at a time when no one else is in the room. I think they really wanted to do it that way as well. Tad didn't really want anyone in the room when he was tracking his guitar stuff.

TAD KUBLER: The record took a long time to make, and I think the longer we took, the worse it got. We definitely needed somebody that was going to say, "What the fuck are you guys doing?" and unfortunately we didn't have that.

CRAIG FINN: I was trying to do something a little different. In some ways "Hurricane J" is creepy. But it's also a little more tender. The thing about *Heaven Is Whenever* is kind of funny. Galen and I always riff on this kind of thing and we came up with this idea of the cosmic philosopher, a hippie-ish rock and roller, Jerry Garcia type, who comes up with homespun truths with a little psychedelic edge. I kept writing these lyrics from the idea of me being a cosmic philosopher. The idea of our fifth album, and suddenly feeling like an elder statesman, had me thinking, *Well, what do you do when you're an elder statesman? You become this cosmic philosopher, and you dole out this advice.* A lot of that record has this weird advice tone. I don't think I was in a place to be giving anyone advice, but there's this kind of advice that's going on, and that's weird. If I ever catch myself doing it now, I try not to, because it does have this obnoxious older-brother feeling.

TAD KUBLER: I don't know what the fuck we were going for production-wise, because it sounds ridiculous. In fact, the guitars at points don't even sound like they're being played through an amp. But I think there are a lot of good ideas there. I think there are a lot of really solid ideas there that we just didn't allow to evolve.

CRAIG FINN: One of the pressures of this time—whether real or imagined—which haunted us for the next few years, was the idea that we'd become a professional band. We were all living off of it. And I think we sometimes made decisions based on what would make us not have to go get jobs again. And that's a terrible way to think: it almost ensures that your work is going to suffer, because the stuff that people really liked is when you didn't even think anyone would hear it. We were doing things both consciously and subconsciously to keep out there, and it didn't really work or it wasn't successful. I love "The Sweet Part of the City." I love "The Weekenders." But the first four records were all really fun to make. The fifth was not, and I feel like you can hear that. It's cold.

GEOFF TRAVIS: It was a little bit of a disappointment. Not crushing, but it felt like their level was dipping. I think that was the main factor in our not renewing. The other stuff we were blissfully ignorant of.

BOBBY DRAKE: Through *Heaven*, I was thinking, *Oh God, I can't do this anymore.* But I knew in my gut it wasn't the end.

TAD KUBLER: I had a problem for about eighteen months, on and off. It's impossible to

do on tour, you think you've got everything planned out: *We're gonna be gone for two weeks, and this is how much I'll need.* And then in four days, you're out of shit. Then you're into some really sketchy business. You're disappearing at all hours, walking around Vancouver. I would do this thing where I would go into tattoo shops, and I would get a tattoo and I would say: "I'm gonna walk around after sound check; what neighborhoods do I want to stay out of?" So I fucking make a beeline right there, which is dangerous.

That lasted for a little bit more than a year, and then I was just like, *I can't keep doing this. It's exhausting.* I went to rehab. I did an outpatient rehab thing at Hazleton. Hazleton has a branch in New York. And I went Monday through Friday, every day from ten to six, for two months. Then I went to meetings and started to get into the recovery community, which is super helpful, and which I'm still a part of. I think I'm just at a different place in my life now, thankfully. It's always something you have to watch out for. Because it's fucking sneaky.

CRAIG FINN: I worked on the reissue of *Heaven Is Whenever* a lot. It's our funniest record. There's a lot of funny lines on it, which is kind of weird because they're not paired with joy. So it doesn't come off that way, but on paper it looks as if this is funny. So given that, it also gave us an opportunity, when we started to play these songs live, to ask, "Well, what if Steve and Franz were in the band when we were doing this? How would that have been?" Great. And I bet you that would have ended up with a way stronger record, because we would have had better personalities.

Dan Neustadt, who played keyboards, is a very nice guy. And it did not work out. Our manager said—it was kind of a business thing—"You aren't going to cut these guys in who come in after four records. So you're gonna have to kind of arrange it as a hired-gun sitch." We're coming off *Stay Positive*, we're starting this new record, we replaced Franz with two people. And then that made our crew bigger too. We actually picked up an extra crew member. So all of a sudden it was kind of a joke. Some of the shows were great, some were not, but I remember right around that time going out and doing a West Coast tour that was B markets. Right around that time I'd realized that we were stronger on the East Coast, no matter what. We'd go into some of these places, college towns with a potentially younger audience, and it wasn't happening. Chico, California, was not showing up for The Hold Steady. Well, we're still doing great in Chicago, and San Francisco and Los Angeles are fine. But we are probably not going to draw an audience of twenty-year-olds anywhere. What do we do?

There were some shifts that needed to be made. One was that after nine months, with a keyboard player who wasn't exactly working, we just let him go. Which allowed us to kill a crew member too. And that left us without a keyboard player, but with a tight group, a tighter group of people that we all felt good about.

TEN

CLICKS AND HISSES AND COMPLICATED CODING

BY MATTHEW HESS

IN A STUFFY DIGITAL MEDIA LAB (SMELLING FAINTLY OF TACO BELL and feet) on the Northeastern University campus in Boston, I began writing the first lines of code that would serve as a fledgling prototype for clicksandhisses.com. This was back in 2012. At the time, my goal was to create something simple and interactive that would allow users to click through The Hold Steady's lyric sheet, exploring the web of references and callbacks. The annotations themselves were an afterthought. I just pulled a few sentences from Wikipedia and submitted the clunky code base as a capstone project for a degree I was finishing.

While the final product was kind of a mess, I still loved the concept: a comprehensive, interactive guide to the Hold Steady discography. It stuck with me like Party City two-sided tape.

As the years passed, my web-development skills improved to a level passable enough to give Clicks and Hisses another try. While I worked on the tech in my spare time, I recruited my good buddy Ray Gradale to add his snarky, effortless flow to a first set of annotations. He augmented my original vision for the site by focusing not only on the dense references in Craig's lyrics, but also on the songs' themes and narratives. When he ran out of gas and retreated to his hammock to scratch dog ears, I took over the annotations to push the project through its initial release. Later on, music blogger/dad Casey Richard pinch hit on a song, and author David Kallison came onboard to lend his literary bona fides to the project as the principal annotator, allowing me to focus on the architecture and design of the site.

This all brings us to what Clicks and Hisses is today. Jay-Z has Tidal, Dolly Parton has Dollywood, but only The Hold Steady has a fan-made, interactive discography platform. A true labor of love, we've annotated almost every song that's been recorded by the band, including bonus tracks, B sides, and rarities. Every annotation is categorized, searchable, and filterable. Every annotation has an image (for better or worse). Every annotation has a fairly consistent approach, with elements of research, speculation, and personal connection (along with some *Pop-Up Video* irreverence). We also compiled the celebrated Hold Steady map.

That being said, the project is not meant to be definitive. We make an effort to uncover what these songs mean, but we also want to communicate what these songs mean to *us* and where the content takes our imaginations. We hope that this approach keeps the site informative, but also

enjoyable to read—and there is a lot to read. So in honor of The Hold Steady's twentieth anniversary, we've compiled twenty of our favorite annotations. As always, we hope that this list sparks some deeper interest in this great band and their songs.

1. *"Holding hands and going steady"—from "Positive Jam"*

Holding hands and going steady basically means dating, not to be confused with holding steady (something sniffling indie kids and clustered-up clever kids should strongly consider doing). Going steady is what teenagers did in the 1950s. Flappers were out, monogamous chicks and root beer floats were in. Maybe after a crippling depression and devastating war, society just wanted to chill out and simplify things. But not for too long. *(Ray)*

2. *"People call me one-hour photo"—from "The Swish"*

The '90s and early '00s were a dark time before you could take a picture of yourself sans-pants and instantly text it unsolicited to your—or your friend's—nonplussed girlfriend. Back then, rolls of film needed to be taken to a developer and therefore people stuck to taking pictures of landscapes. The one-hour-photo guy would turn your crappy attempts at becoming a photographer into something your mom could begrudgingly magnet to the fridge. The idea of a guy working with dangerous chemicals in a dark room to satiate and profit off your stupid hobby/habit easily lends itself to the drug-induced story line we are currently exploring. *(Ray)*

3. *"You gotta make do with what they gave to you"—from "You Gotta Dance (With Who You Came to the Dance With)"*

This is either referring to drugs and alcohol—you have to settle for whatever skunk beer is available at your cousin's house party—or the genetic hand you were dealt, i.e., your looks and their correlation to your ability to pick up someone at said house party. *(David)*

4. *"Whoever's gonna get me the highest"—from "Hornets! Hornets!"*

The legs on this running double entendre pick up where they left off on *Almost Killed Me* with Holly's incompatible pursuit of faith and Feminax—her two great hopes for salvation. This line explains her morals, simultaneously loose and lofty. She will have to go with the guy who will give her the best trip, the religion that will give her the best shot at a rebirth, and ultimately whichever of the two can lead her to a resurrection. One could say she's seeking a new life, a new first day of the rest of her life—a "separation Sunday," if you will. *(Ray)*

5. *"People touching people they don't even know"—from "Hornets! Hornets!"*

Craig does one of those scalp-tingling things here, where he takes Holly's backstory and her pain and brings in Kate Bush's fantastical cure of having people swap places so they won't treat each other so coldly. Then he jumps into the song to remind listeners that at big rock shows people from all different backgrounds let their guard down and touch each other's lives, maybe swapping pills or smooches instead of places, but nonetheless partially acting out the deal in "Running Up That Hill." *(Ray)*

6. *"Cross around her neck"—from "Cattle and the Creeping Things"*

A lot to unpack here. The most clear reference is to the Christian symbol of Jesus dying on the cross. Here, we dive deeper into Holly literally bearing the cross, another cliché referring to a personal struggle one must carry through life, born from Jesus carrying said cross before being nailed to it. But it doesn't stop there, as Holly's cross is stolen—reflecting on her somewhat shitty life choices (stealing a Christian girl's cross)—and the fact that a well-to-do girl born into opportunity has stolen the life story of a down-on-her-luck girl who came from nothing. Holly's cross to bear is not her own; she went out and created the dark situation she is in, for love of drama and self-pity and, ultimately, a way to make her life feel interesting. *(Ray)*

7. *"Wore a cross to ward them off"—from "Banging Camp"*

This continues the overdramatization of life that Holly promotes to escape what she sees as her basic bitch upbringing. In her teenage mind, townie cops are as serious as biblical plagues or vamps, and she is their badass target. That said, she is probably correct that a girl rocking a cross is less likely to get searched. The dichotomy for Holly continues, at once embracing her new risky lifestyle while at the same time clinging to the useful parts of her upbringing. The string and cross are her lifelines back to a time she hasn't completely abandoned. *(Ray)*

8. "Stumbled into the foyer and pulled the bookshelf over / We were drowning in the literature" —from "The Most Important Thing"
This verse almost reads like some sort of Hold Steady genesis story. We have a friend group of guys, a noise-rock track ("She Blows Blasts of Static") blending with classic Americana (*Music from Big Pink*), a songwriter struck by horror fantasy (Bram Stoker), beat poetry (Allen Ginsberg), a Bible—all elements of Craig's songwriting. After drowning in the literature (a sort of lyrical baptism), the band is resurrected. Overlooked indie rockers (Lifter Puller) are born again as The Hold Steady—America's favorite goddamn bar band. *(Matt)*

9. "We had some massive nights, every song was right"—from "Massive Nights"
Sometimes when you're partying, the stars align and everything just seems to click. The weather is comfortable. You've calibrated your inebriation perfectly. The clientele is the right mix, everyone is having a good time, and your attractive neighbor is stealing glances at you. The playlist is straight fire. The party goes wild when the live version of "Dance Yrself Clean" drops into that first, filthy bassline. Everyone nods and grooves and lets you know they're on the same level. You couldn't get there every night, but when you did it was a beautiful thing. *(Matt)*

10. "I never saw that girl/boy again"—from "Chillout Tent"
There's something to be said for an intense, fleeting romance. Even if it was just for an evening. Even if it was medically supervised. There's no baggage or extended history to ruin it after the fact. It can exist in a vacuum. It remains pristine. The lovers are left only with fond memories of that strange corner of time when they were young and sexy and felt that an authentic, instant connection with someone was still possible. It's worth noting that this song may present the least sad time that boys and girls in America have together. At least on this album anyway. *(Matt)*

11. "To be perfectly honest, they didn't seem much different"—from "One for the Cutters"
Like many college students, the girl has some preconceived notions about townie boys. Their looks. Their style. Their demeanor. "One for the Cutters" offers some commentary on the "town and gown" dynamic of Bloomington, Indiana—the relationship between the nonacademic community (town) and the university community (gown). The girl keeps her late-night activities a secret from

her friends and family. They would likely consider the townies as uneducated, unrefined, and dangerous. A bunch of flyover-state rubes. The townies likely see the students as stiff, elitist, and out of touch. A bunch of uppity douchebags from Zionsville. However, the lyrics take care to mention several times that *"he didn't seem that different."* Craig often points out that despite our backgrounds and geography, we have more in common than we realize. *"We all want the same things"*—drinking heavily outdoors apparently being one of those things. *(Matt)*

12. "She gets pretty wasted at the celebrations / The benefits and the building dedications"—from "Magazines"

Magazine Girl is invited to high-society events like benefits and building dedications. She slinks into a black cocktail dress, tees up a tasteful amount of cleavage, and hits the open bar. She gets hammered at these things. Who needs to develop a sense of personal accountability when you have impeccable cheekbones? It hasn't ruined her so far, and even the narrator dismisses her behavior, blaming it on daddy issues and the heavy New York scene. *(Matt)*

13. "But it's not gonna be like in romantic comedies / In the end I bet no one learns a lesson"—from "The Weekenders"

The narrator offers his own premonition: Their story will not be tied up with a neat little bow. There will not be a happily-ever-after, guy-gets-the-girl, long-soft-kiss-in-the-street-as-the-wind-swirls-leaves-around romantic-comedy ending. He doubts that she'll be able to reel in her powers

after a taste of the fast life. He doubts that she'll settle down and be faithful to him as a stable, loyal partner. He even asks her to "keep it decent" if they want to continue seeing each other. He doesn't want to fall back into that trap. It seems that someone actually did learn a lesson. *(Matt)*

14. "Hurricane Jesse's gonna crash into the harbor this summer"—from "Hurricane J"
I find this line particularly interesting. The narrator spends much of the song reflecting on how the scene churns up young waitresses, leaving them hardened and haggard and hacking with a loud, wet smoker's cough. By describing Jesse as a hurricane crashing into the harbor, he's suggesting a few things: 1) *She's* the one to worry about. 2) *She's* the one imposing her will. 3) Jesse has the potential intensity to crash into the scene, leaving it broken and scattered like storm debris. Not the other way around. In this sense, the song may be an extended way for him to tune out the realization that he just can't handle her, even if he wants to. As the National Ocean Service tells us: there's never been a Hurricane Jessica before. *(Matt)*

15. "For me, it was mostly the music"—from "I Hope This Whole Thing Didn't Frighten You"
I'd like to think this lyric is autobiographical. Craig Finn was a witness to some amazing things. Growing up with Prince's stranglehold of the Twin Cities region (assuming that was in the background), he was also able to see the Replacements when he was in junior high and high school. As

a believable band of normal people, the Replacements made rock and roll attainable to the average kid who didn't look and strut like Mick Jagger. They also had the balls to call their record *Let It Be*. Along with the 'Ments, Craig was able to see Hüsker Dü and Soul Asylum throughout high school before moving to Boston for college in the late '80s—which had an amazing scene including the Pixies, Dinosaur Jr., Morphine, Mission of Burma, and of course Bel Biv Devoe. Quite the formative experience in the pre-Internet dark ages. *(Casey)*

16. "Let's get on with the business"—from "On with the Business"

This song is largely based on ideas put forth by David Foster Wallace in his hipster bible, *Infinite Jest*. (Actually, *Jest* is often considered a masterwork of the literary '90s; alternately, it's been called "watching someone wave their dick around all over the page.") *(David)*

17. "That same stupid feeling but he likes his new haircut"—from "Denver Haircut"

I was once glued up on a woman who just didn't love me back. I told my hairdresser I wanted something radical, something crazy. She refused. "Nothing on the outside ever fixes the inside," she said. Wise woman. *(David)*

18. "You did good kid"—from "You Did Good Kid"

When a stand-up comedian gets offstage, whether they killed or bombed, the other comedians will often just say, "You did good, kid." Throughout the song, the main character is constantly reminded of this middling, noncommittal noncompliment and its description of his life—never too terrible, but never too great either. *(David)*

19. "Vanilla vodka and a Diet Dr Pepper"—from "Spices"

Dr Pepper is a carbonated soda drink created in Waco, Texas, around 1885. It is, without question, the greatest soda of all time and one of Texas's most important exports. The diet version was first released in the early '60s as Dietetic Dr Pepper. Consumers thought it was only for diabetics (where were the *Mad Men* boys on this one?). The name was changed to Sugar Free Dr Pepper and then finally, in 1987, it became Diet Dr Pepper. Also, no offense, but this sounds like a terrible cocktail. *(David)*

20. "Blasting out through built-in speakers like it's bug spray"—from "Family Farm"

To hear Van Halen's "Eruption" (such beauty, such raditude) be shat out of a phone's speakers like a wet fart is sacrilegious, regardless of how you feel about the Lord. *(David)*

ELEVEN

PARTY FAVORS TO PARTY SAVIORS

TAD KUBLER: Steve Selvidge joining saved the band.

CRAIG FINN: Steve was in a band called the Bloodthirsty Lovers and they had come from the Grifters, a Memphis band I really loved. So much that I got to know them a little bit and tagged along on a couple of dates when I was on the East Coast, and then also they'd stay at my house in Minneapolis and I think Lifter Puller played with them. When the Grifters split up, Dave Shouse started the Bloodthirsty Lovers, and we shared an agent.

TAD KUBLER: We met Steve on the first tour we ever did. We were touring down to South by Southwest, and on the way down there, we connected with the Bloodthirsty Lovers. He was fucking rail thin, he had cowboy boots on, Wranglers, and a white T-shirt—that was all I ever saw him in. And his hair was massive. Watching Steve play was mind-blowing. Maybe the second or third show, we were playing like this weird art gallery in Alabama. They didn't have a bar or anything like that, and we were looking around, and I'm like, "They don't serve alcohol here." Panic. Steve was standing next to me, and at the same time we both pulled out a pint of whiskey from our back pocket. It was kind of like, *Great minds think alike!* So we sound-checked and then both bands had something to eat and were drinking, and Steve and I were talking about skateboarding, and he was like, "Well, when were you born?" and I was like, "June of '73," and he was like "No way, what day?" and I said, "June 29."

STEVE SELVIDGE (GUITARIST, THE HOLD STEADY): I was like, "That's my birthday too!" And so we both pulled out our licenses, you know, to prove it to one another, and as touring was back in those days, I had a pint of Jack Daniel's in my back pocket, and I was like, I grabbed it to say, "We should cheers about that," and he had a pint of Jim Beam in his back pocket, and without knowing what I was doing, did the same thing, so at the same time, we both pulled out our pints of whiskey and were just best buds ever since.

CRAIG FINN: He was definitely Tad's friend. When we were touring, if we went through Memphis, Tad would call Steve.

STEVE SELVIDGE: I'm sitting at home and, as I remember it, Tad texted me: *Hey, man* *what are you doing?* I'm like, *Nothing, I'm just at home. Well, our gig in New Orleans fell through, we're driving to Memphis, we're going to have a drinking contest with Lucero,* and I was like, *All right, that sounds awesome.* There's this really grubby, seedy after-hours bar called the Buccaneer, and so we went there and, you know, I didn't really have a dog in the hunt, because I wasn't in either band at that point, so I was just there to hang out with some friends.

CRAIG FINN: We were in New Orleans, and I'd gone out. I think I met a friend for breakfast. I remember getting done with breakfast and going back to the truck and just thinking, *We have a day off today, we just have to drive to our show, wherever that is.* I think the show was in Little Rock. *But all we have to do is drive to the show. And I'm going to go to the hotel, and I'm going to get some sleep that I so desperately need. And tonight I'm not going to drink.* And I got up to the van and those guys were all at it. And Tad yelled, "We're driving to Memphis to have a drinking contest with Lucero!" And I thought, *Oh my God.* But we did.

STEVE SELVIDGE: I don't know what the criteria for winning was. I know that Lucero, in my experience, tended to throw up a lot, whereas The Hold Steady maybe not so much. I think my wife Joann dropped me off and I just sat there and drank a lot, and then at some point she just came and picked me up. It was great. And who knows what happened in between?

CRAIG FINN: Tad really had him in mind when Franz left. He said, "Well, what are we going to do? We should have a guitar player also." And he right away put in for Steve, which we all thought was a good idea. We were really touring a ton and it didn't bother me at all that he didn't live in town, because we were always on the move. If Steve wanted to do it, we were all pretty good with him.

TAD KUBLER: When it came time to have a serious talk about adding another guitar player, we had a short list of people, and Steve was near the top. There was concern about him living in Memphis, but we had become friends with enough other bands that didn't all live in the same city and realized that it could be done. So we asked three people, and Steve was the most excited about it, and my first choice anyways.

STEVE SELVIDGE: It was around November of 2009, I was in the studio at Ardent, and I get a call from Tad, and I'm like, "Hey, what's up?" He's like, "Man, Franz left and this is new territory for us. We're going to have to get another keyboard player. If we're going to have a hired-gun keyboard player, I'd like to get a second guitar player, just to fill things out, and you were one of the first people I thought about. Is it something you'd be interested in doing?" I was like, "Yes, absolutely! That'd be great!" I didn't hear from him for months after that. Then in February, he called me again. On March 28, I left Memphis to go start the *Heaven Is Whenever* album cycle. I was waiting for Joann to get out of the bathroom so she could take me to the airport, and she walked out and said, "I'm pregnant." "Great! We've been trying to get pregnant for a while now, that's great, I'll see you in July."

TAD KUBLER: When Steve came in, I created a tremendous amount of space for him. In hindsight, I created the space for Steve that I should have created for Franz and never did.

GALEN POLIVKA: His father was a musician, and he was of that world, surrounded by musicians his whole life, and he knew how to acclimate. What was actually quite fun for me was that he took the view, *The piano player left so I'll reinterpret those parts as guitar parts.* So at rehearsals it was fun: it wasn't an entirely new band for me, but he would emphasize things that Franz wouldn't, and vice versa. And that kept me on my toes in a way that was interesting and fun. Steve's a wildly dexterous musician who can do anything, basically. It was interesting, fun, and challenging, all at the same time.

CRAIG FINN: I think we would have broken up without him. I'm not exaggerating. The fact that he was very good friends with Tad, who was most likely to go off and be his own island and maybe sometimes feel frustrated or not appreciated—Steve was able to help that. He'd been on

the road a lot. He comes from a musician family. I think he very much understood the gig, how to not be needy, and not make waves as a new guy, just do the gig and figure out the gig.

STEVE SELVIDGE: They were struggling. I know that situation when the right breath of fresh air comes in; it really changes things and it gives you a new lease on life, and we just had a great time, so I think that sustained us for a while. And I'll take that: I'm glad to have played that part.

CRAIG FINN: He was a calming presence that we really needed and appreciated. Tad wasn't threatened by him in the way that he had been by Franz. There was no writing for Steve to be doing at that point, he was just playing. And Steve writes, but he's not a super-prolific writer. So I think there was that. The other thing that really was a part of the band in this era was that I was getting a lot more attention than anyone. And that was a problem. That was something we talked about a lot and management was talking to me about. There was a lot of that sentiment. I think that every band goes through it. But after getting Franz out of there, Steve wasn't going to be threatening. No one was going to be paying too much attention to the new guy.

STEVE SELVIDGE: The biggest thing was literally navigating where I was standing, because Franz had been stage right, downstage, and that's where I was standing. I felt like there was a faction of people who were really bummed that Franz was gone, and maybe not super open to seeing someone else there. And keep in mind, too, that when I joined the band, Tad basically

WHEN I JOINED THE BAND, TAD BASICALLY HAD A MISTER ROGERS VIBE GOING ON—LOTS OF CARDIGANS, SHORT HAIR—AND I LOOKED LIKE A BEAST

had a Mister Rogers vibe going on—lots of cardigans, short hair—and I looked like a beast. My hair was past my shoulders, I had a giant beard; it was certainly incongruous.

TAD KUBLER: One of the things that bothered me was the narrative of the band; it seemed a little one-sided. And it bothered me because for the band to work, everybody's got to feel good about contributing. After all is said and done, that's my only issue with it, but I don't think that's anything Craig had anything to do with necessarily.

FRANZ NICOLAY: It's like an old marriage: they're stuck with each other, like Mick and Keith. It's really a classic, archetypal rock relationship: these two guys who have this creative partnership going back decades. I think they're fine with each other now, but they definitely gripe about each other. They've come to an understanding; they understand each other extremely well. I read Tad say something about Craig once which I thought was extremely insightful, which is that Craig has a very deep well of empathy for strangers but that he is not always great at extending this to people who are close to him. And I think that's correct. I also think it's something that he's gotten a lot better at.

Craig's dad was the CFO of a major corporation, and so he has a businessman's view of the world in many ways. And he's not very comfortable—or *was* not, I think, again, less so now—addressing hurt feelings or anything that would require an emotional investment in the people around him, or in him from the people around him. He's just super uncomfortable with it. And I remember being confused about him in the old days because he was obviously a reader and intellectual and an artistic person, but I didn't see that. I never saw him reading books, we never talked about books. I got the impression of him as the nerdy guy who's learned to hang out with the jocks by hiding the intellectual parts of himself, or the parts of himself that are artistically curious or emotionally curious, and that his outlet for that was in his lyrics. But his public presen-

tation with people was the way that he had learned to hang with Midwestern dudes, which was the sports stuff, the drinking stuff, the party stuff: that was a barrier in front of the artistic core of this guy. He's a Midwestern Catholic: he's not extremely emotionally accessible.

TAD KUBLER: You know, I tried talking to Craig about it a couple of times. And I'm sure I didn't go about it the right way. And after that, it just dropped. I don't think Craig has gotten any attention that isn't incredibly well deserved. In hindsight, you're able to have this kind of perspective, but at the time, I know I wasn't able to, which certainly did some damage to the band and to my relationship with Craig. But he's the lead singer, and that's always the way it goes. It's just how it is.

At the end of the day, I think if your expectations exceed what your gratitude is, any kind of situation you're going to have problems. Ringo Starr will always be my favorite Beatle. One, because his look was unstoppable. Two, he's a much better drummer than anybody ever gives him credit for. And three, he realized that he was in the presence of greatness and he was grateful to be there. I'm sure he had his ups and downs and problems with those guys and with the band and everything else, but he seemed to really have his head around his role. And it took me a long time to figure that out. That's why I don't really do a ton of press anymore. Craig's got that handled. He does a much better interview than I would ever hope to. He also has the narrative in mind constantly. And I'm sure the drugs and alcohol weren't helpful to any of that.

BOBBY DRAKE: There was a lot of baggage on Kubler's end. He knows he fucked up hard.

CRAIG FINN: The ending of the touring of *Heaven Is Whenever* was kind of rough. It didn't feel like Tad was in a good place. We were kind of limping home. And it wasn't as much fun.

TAD KUBLER: I wasn't using drugs anymore, but I may as well have been, because I probably would have been more pleasant to be around. I didn't know how to do it without getting loaded, and it took me a long time to figure it out. One of the things about bands that makes them so volatile is that you rely on everybody to bring their best selves to the band, and when they can't, you do what you can to be supportive and to try and help them figure out how to do that. But there's only so much other people are able to do. So when one person is going through whatever it is, everybody goes through it, and that's not an easy thing to be a part of or to watch.

STEVE SELVIDGE: At the end of 2010, we decided to continue without a keyboard player, which is pretty baffling if you really think about it. If you have two hired guns and you're The Hold Steady and you're going to get rid of one, you probably wouldn't get rid of the keyboard player, but yet they chose to stick with me.

GALEN POLIVKA: All of a sudden, the big break in "Stuck Between Stations," we'll just skip that. Even at the time, we thought, *We should probably figure something out here*. It's not that it didn't occur to us, obviously. Certain songs that were really good were all of a sudden not in the set. It wasn't an unmitigated disaster—the live show was still good enough—but if you take any band and you take a major songwriting and stage presence away, it's going to be different. And nine times out of ten, it's probably going to be somewhat compromised.

STEVE SELVIDGE: God bless them, the people that stuck with us through those times. They didn't get exactly what they came for.

CRAIG FINN: I was writing a lot of songs, which I was trying to bring in. And there's a weird thing about The Hold Steady, which is a number of times I've brought in something where it's like, "Here's a few chords, and I've got this great lyric that I'm really proud of. So let's turn it into a song." And we couldn't really do that. We couldn't really focus. I've always had a hard time focusing Tad on making music in that direction—it has to come from a riff or something that starts with him. So I had all these songs piling up, and I was like, *I think I'd just like to make a record. I want to make that solo record.* We took a little time off.

GALEN POLIVKA: We were coming back from Australia and Craig was like, "Could you come down a half hour early for lobby call—it's nothing heavy, but I just want to talk to you guys." He said, "My new solo record's coming out, and I'm gonna tour it properly. We're going to be on hiatus for six to eight months."

It was kind of welcome, frankly. That spring and summer was probably the first spring and summer I'd been home for four or five years. It was time to step away from it for a second and I think if we wouldn't have, it wouldn't have been productive. It would have been a waste of time. We just needed the time apart to get back together again in a healthy environment really. It was unhealthy enough to not be productive. And if it's neither fun nor productive, why are we doing this? Let's just let the dust settle and figure out where we are. Craig's solo career kept him occupied and it left us individually to get in the headspace to regroup.

TAD KUBLER: I definitely thought, *All right, Craig's had enough.*

STEVE SELVIDGE: That's always going to be in the back of your mind. I mean, that's the dynamic from time immemorial: the frontman doesn't want to do it anymore.

TAD KUBLER: But on a personal level, it allowed me to really spend time with my daughter at a time in her life when it was crucial. Things happened the way they needed to, and I'm grateful for that in a lot of ways, because I wouldn't have the relationship with Murphy that I do now had we gone back out on tour for two years. That's not something I would ever be able to get back. And I started doing some other work which I think had sort of rebuilt my confidence.

CRAIG FINN: I was really excited about the opportunity [to make a solo record]. I remember having some meeting where those guys were expressing concern, and I was just like, "Look, man, we've been doing a lot of this. I just want to do something different. It'll be fun, it'll be good for me." And it really was. It really was positive for me as a musician, as a songwriter. Having a producer being like, "Okay, these are four guys. Shake all their hands, and then show them the first song we're gonna do." And to come out five days later with a full record, saying, "This doesn't need to be so difficult. You just learn the songs and play them." There's a lot of stuff in a band that makes it a lot harder. And we'd gotten a little bit bloated with The Hold Steady at that point. We couldn't write and record unless Dusty was there, the guitar tech, to set up the stuff. Well, that has nothing to do with the song. I can write a song on a nylon-stringed guitar missing a string. I think it was a little [worrying to the others] but it kind of felt like it got squashed quickly.

TAD KUBLER: Craig's solo thing, I think, was one of the best things that he could have done as well, because it did give him a lot of perspective on the personalities that you have to deal with

in a band. That's the one thing I think I've noticed the most about working with Craig now, in Hold Steady 2.0 or whatever we're calling it at this point.

CRAIG FINN: I was helped, I think musically and creatively, by the solo tour. It also allowed me to realize how the dynamic of a band is difficult. When Pavement broke up, Malkmus said, "A band is the worst idea ever." Yeah. There was something about just playing music with people and having a hierarchy: "I'm Craig Finn, I'm gonna pay you money, you're gonna play the music, and then when we go home, you're gonna go away, and I'm not gonna be responsible for you." A band is better than a sum of its parts if it's good. But I wasn't feeling we were in that place where we were better than the sum of our parts. We were unwieldy. We had one of the main members living out of town, we were flying him in, it took us a long time to get the songs together. We changed management during that time. After going so hard for so many years, we had taken some time off, and the momentum wasn't there. It was a struggle.

STEVE SELVIDGE: Look, I was joining the band in 2010, starting to work on writing stuff in 2011, then by 2012 we still haven't started recording a record. I knew that that wasn't exactly standard operating procedure and it wasn't the best thing.

GALEN POLIVKA: Especially with Franz not there, Craig and Tad were the creative engines of the band. It seemed to me that their history is so long and they had issues to work out amongst themselves. And until they did, I was just waiting for them to figure things out, to see

THEIR MIDWESTERN ROOTS MEAN ON THE SURFACE THAT EVERYTHING IS ALWAYS FINE. AND UNDERNEATH, THEY'RE NOT SHARING.

whether this band even existed anymore, basically. It was unspoken: *We've just got to sit on our hands for a second and wait till everybody comes up for air and see what we want to do.* It was a difficult time for everybody.

DAVID GOTTLIEB (MANAGER, THE HOLD STEADY): I knew The Hold Steady's lawyer, George Regis, from going to New York Rangers hockey games. And over the next few years, George and I would randomly discuss things at games. He would ask me questions about how I approach certain things with management. And there were even a couple of times where Craig came to games, and I met him and got to talk to him. And then one day in late 2012, George called me up and said, "Would you like to manage The Hold Steady? Because they're making a change. They're talking to some people and you're on the list." I said, "Okay." And so we had a couple of meetings, and at some point late in 2012, I met them all at a bar downtown, and that was apparently my acceptance as manager. They were not in a good state, and I did not know the depths of that state. At that moment, my knowledge of them was that they were road warriors and successful road warriors. I remember we had some ideas, and whatever conversations we had, I felt confident enough in their direction at that moment that whatever I could contribute would only help execute that.

CRAIG FINN: After Tad got sick, we set up the business so we were going to get a monthly salary, everyone.

DAVID GOTTLIEB: That was just unaffordable.

CRAIG FINN: And we were going to pay for health insurance.

DAVID GOTTLIEB: In America for a small business, that's a significant expense. Everybody had health insurance because everybody needed it. So it's not a bad thing that people had health insurance, it's just expensive. And one member of the band in particular liked to buy a lot of gear. They had a whole storage space in Ireland with our bus company that was holding a duplicate set of live touring gear.

CRAIG FINN: So during this period there was a lot of taking shows to make payroll. The agent would say, "Well, you got this festival offer in Florida." And you'd say, "Well, look at that, that looks absolutely hellish and terrible." And then they'd say, "Yeah, well, here's what it pays." And we'd say, "Book the flights, we're doing it." And so you're playing a lot of shows that are sucking the life out of you.

DAVID GOTTLIEB: The biggest surprise was that they had no money. And when I say they had no money, they had x in the bank, and they had y debts that were more than x in the bank. It didn't necessarily scare me, it was just like, *Okay, we need to start looking under some rocks and figuring out some ways to get money.* Surprisingly, some things happened pretty quickly. The *Game of Thrones* opportunity happened within two months of when Jeroen van der Meer and I started to manage the band. And that helps. The band began work on demos of new music. And we did a few other things to minimize some of the band's expenses.

CRAIG FINN: I had started to think about how I could be a leader, a benevolent leader, rather than act like every decision is going to be made as a group. Because to be honest, not everyone wants to be involved in all the decision-making, as long as the decisions are being made well, and not putting people in discomfort or distress.

DAVID GOTTLIEB: It was quickly apparent that The Hold Steady had two leaders in Tad and Craig, and that they were also trying to be a democracy. And if there's one thing I've learned in this, it's that democracies don't work in rock bands, for a variety of reasons. Any experience I'd had before on both the label side and as a manager definitely backs that up. Democracies don't work and there needs to be a leader, and in this case we had two. Craig and Tad certainly had different thoughts on things. Their Midwestern roots mean on the surface that everything is always fine. And underneath, they're not sharing. That was certainly apparent. Tad was still in the early stages of physically and mentally recovering from his medical issues and his addiction issues. So that made things a little awkward at times between Craig and Tad.

TAD KUBLER: Craig's break from the band ended up being the better part of a year, so his idea was, "You guys can keep working on songs and just send me demos." So we did, and, well, we all know how that went.

CRAIG FINN: While I was on tour for the solo record, they actually went to Memphis and tried to work on some music. Some of those songs became songs. With the two guitars, it was all so dense that when I heard it, I couldn't figure out where to put myself in it. It's easier for me to start with something a little sparse or a little more wide open. And the shit I was coming up with wasn't that strong. I didn't really have a vision for it. And it all sounded too hard rock to me, to be honest. So you know, if there's rock and roll and then there's hard rock, it was too hard rock. Everything seemed a little lumbering.

STEVE SELVIDGE: Say what you will about *Teeth Dreams*, but Tad and Bobby and Galen came down to Memphis and we just holed up in my studio at my house and we wrote and we wrote and we wrote, and it was really great. I mean, it was a fantastic time. And I mean, it felt good to me creatively, and it felt good to be hanging with them, and it just felt good to have them in my own town. That was really validating to me. And initially Craig was like, "Cool, man, love what we're hearing," and it wasn't until later that he was like, "I can't find a way into any of these songs." But I think that was the first time we had worked separately; I think that's the first time he received a chunk of music that he hadn't been a part of.

CRAIG FINN: We kept trying to write. We'd get Steve in town but it was kind of stilted. Before, we had the space and Bobby and Tad would go down there and write three songs with a case

of beer. Suddenly, we're flying Steve into town, we're going into a rehearsal studio, we're all staring at each other: "Okay." "Right." And there wasn't much flow to it. I remember one time, I was like, "Let's go down to Asbury Park." We had access to a house. Like, "Let's just go down there with acoustics." We ended up going down there and just partying. It wasn't that inspiring of a time.

DAVID GOTTLIEB: When Vagrant decided to pass on the option and Rough Trade decided to pass on the option in the UK, we had to find them a new home. In 2013, that was where a lot of the time was spent. We were on the verge of signing with one label, when somebody came in at the eleventh hour and basically said, "What do you want?" Instead of, "Here's what we have," which is where we had been with everybody else. And I told them and they didn't blink. And they said okay. So I had a meeting with the guys and said, "Well, if you want to make the record that you're talking about making, and you want to put some money in your pocket from a record deal, then you should do this. And if you don't, if you want to continue at the level you're at, we can do that, and then you should go with the other label that feels more emotionally invested." And we chose Razor and Tie because Razor and Tie wrote a very big check.

GALEN POLIVKA: *Teeth Dreams* was not a hugely fun record to make. I don't think the material was as strong as it could have been. And every record isn't everybody's best record. If you put out nine records, they're not all going to be mind-blowing, and *Teeth Dreams* is not a mind-blowing record. Again, there's songs on there that I like, but it's the same kind of thing as *Heaven Is Whenever*, but without life-threatening illness involved.

CRAIG FINN: It was a struggle. My mother was sick, and she ended up dying in 2013, which is when we finally made the record, that summer. So what I brought to that record, I don't know.

GALEN POLIVKA: Thinking back to that time, we were down in Tennessee, and again it was, "Oh, here's our project, and we're all here to do the same thing." But we were on top of each other. Recording in New York, you're sleeping in your own bed, but this was pretty remote. It was in this place, Franklin, Tennessee, which is a good forty minutes outside of Nashville. So once we are on-site, we're on-site, which in theory is fine. But sometimes you want to go to a bookstore, or just go for a walk, or eat a meal alone.

When we were making *Boys and Girls*, we were in New York, and when we were done recording, we would go for drinks, and then that would turn into, "Where's the song going? Do you think that needs another guitar track?" While we were hanging out, we were also scheming and working in a weird way as well. Whereas when you're on top of each other to begin with, it's, "Oh, we're done for the day? Cool. I just want to go read a magazine or something." Nick, the producer, was a super-fun hang, and got good performances out of us. But not one of our stronger records, and

IF YOU PUT OUT NINE RECORDS, THEY'RE NOT ALL GOING TO BE MIND-BLOWING

not one of the funnest to make. It was encouraging that we did throw together enough material to make a record, but it's not our best record.

BOBBY DRAKE: The recording of it was kinda strange. Tad was pretty freaked out about it.

TAD KUBLER: It felt like another missed opportunity to try and do something great.

CRAIG FINN: Sonically, I still look back on it and say, *Why didn't the producer stop this?* There had been a sense that the rest of the band were wary of "Craig's guys." So I said, "All right, let me not really be involved in choosing the producer." So we had Nick Raskulinecz, who is an accomplished producer. But generally of hard rock records: Rush, Deftones, Foo Fighters. He had a specific way to make records, and I don't think he exactly understood what we were doing. I think he put us into his thing. Really nice guy, really enthusiastic guy, but there's very little variation of tone throughout the record. I think we were kind of checked out. I was there, I was participating. So it's not like, "I didn't make this record." But I wasn't in a great headspace during that record.

DAVID GOTTLIEB: There were a variety of things going on with *Teeth Dreams*. I think Craig ceded most control of making the record to Tad, and Tad wanted to make a big rocker. Especially because this was going to be the second record without Franz. And that's where Nick came in. I happened to know Nick from my time spent with Foo Fighters. And I think the songs are there. I think the record sounds pretty good. I think there is something missing. I can't tell you what that is. It may be as simple as missing Franz. But I think there's some great songs on that record. I think "Oaks" is a top song. Unfortunately, because it's on that record, people don't notice it. It's not to argue it's their best record. But I think they made the right record for the label we had at the time we signed; they didn't make the right record for the label we had after we mastered it, because the label just crumbled.

CRAIG FINN: I remember a lot of nights, especially from 2010 to 2015, thinking, *I don't know if I can do it tonight*, but there's been very, very, very few shows that when I got up onstage,

FUCK, I'M FORTY-ONE YEARS OLD, I'M LUCKY TO BE IN A BAND THIS LONG. BANDS BREAK UP. THIS BAND WILL BREAK UP.

and the music started playing, that I didn't feel pretty excited by it. Unless something was really going weird, it's pretty easy to get there. Once the guitars are on and the amps are on, it's gonna be okay.

CRAIG McQUISTON: It was rough. We were such close friends, but I felt like it had gotten to the point where maybe I shouldn't work for the band anymore. Because in some weird way, I didn't want to be around for the collapse. Because I knew that I couldn't control it. It was rough on some of those tours, because we were playing C and D markets in the States. And everybody got to the point where it was like, *Why are we doing this?* We were in Toledo, Ohio, on a Tuesday night. We were routed to get us back to New York. And I remember Craig asked me, "What's the ticket count for tonight? Is tonight sold out?" We'd have some shows that ticket counts were not that great. And I didn't really want to tell Craig how bad the ticket count was. But it's a rainy night in Toledo, and we're just trying to get back to New York. I remember that night in particular. Galen's mental health had gone down the toilet. And that night really felt like the end. I was like, *I cannot wait to get off this bus and away from the situation.* But everybody was in the same boat. It was really very dark.

STEVE SELVIDGE: I felt like Galen was done, I felt like he was just playing out the string until somebody said, "Okay, you can stop now." And Bobby wasn't in great shape—I mean, maybe nobody was.

CRAIG FINN: While we were touring *Teeth Dreams*, I started making *Faith in the Future* with Josh Kaufman. And that was also a revelation. The first solo record was great. The second one felt very exciting to me, much more exciting than what I was doing in the band at that moment. And so the ease and creativity that was happening in that part of my life was really exciting. There was less ego and demanding attention. It was, "Let's try it this way. Great." "Okay, that didn't work. Let's try it this way." And being excited about that. So I was just gonna keep working.

I didn't think The Hold Steady was over, but I thought we needed a good long break. If I'm being honest, I thought it would probably be good for some people to realize what life would be like without the band and how hard it is to get other things going. And I think lessons were learned on that front. Maybe because I'm a terrible optimist, but I did not think we were done. But I think other people in the band did.

GALEN POLIVKA: I might have been one of the people who thought we were finished, I guess. It was a bit of a slog at that point. It all hinges on Craig and Tad, and if they're in a good place, and they're communicating well, good stuff happens. And when they're not communicating, it doesn't seem like much of anything happens. When they weren't in a position to spend time together, it came to a grinding halt and people just sat on their hands and waited for them, which is testament to it being their thing.

STEVE SELVIDGE: It wasn't until after the *Teeth Dreams* tour, toward the end of that album cycle, which was somewhat truncated, that I really felt, *Okay, this is pretty jacked up.* Nothing could mask the ennui that had set in, so it was like, *All right, well, looks like this band's about* *to break up. Fuck, I'm forty-one years old, I'm lucky to be in a band this long. Bands break up. This band will break up.*

DAVID GOTTLIEB: We played one more show early in 2015, a private event in New York, around the NBA All-Star Game. And we had a band meeting. A few people expressed their displeasure with continuing the way things were going and were just like, "Let's take a break." And that's what happened. So all of 2015 they took a break, and Craig was releasing a solo record. I think Tad was the most blindsided by that. And when I say they took a break, there was *no* Hold Steady business in 2015.

CRAIG FINN: We didn't do anything for over a year.

TAD KUBLER: Craig called me and said, "Deer Tick are in town, I'm going to go to the show: do you want to go?" I remember having plans with my girlfriend and getting off the phone and saying, "Hey, Craig asked me if I wanted to go to a show tonight," and she's like, "You better do that." It was so out of the blue and so weird, I felt like, *Right, this is not about seeing Deer Tick.* So we went, it was fun, we had a good time. And then a week later, he called me again and said, "Hey, I'm going to go to another show." I remember him getting me out of the house three weeks in a row to go see some music, and on the third night we shared a cab back to Brooklyn. As he was getting out, he said, "Hey, do you maybe want to get together and work on some music?" as the car was like pulling away! Classic fucking Craig Finn. Like, "Oh, by the way . . ." "Uh-huh, okay, sure, yeah, call me." And that's sort of how it started.

CRAIG FINN: Maybe 2015 or 2016. I went to see Titus Andronicus. And Patrick Stickles did this thing where he got me onstage and we were supposed to do a Replacements song. But he tricked me and the band went into "Stuck Between Stations" and people went fucking nuts. Later, I did a tour with them and we were playing Webster Hall. He's like, "Do you want to do it?" And I was like, "Yeah, BUT we should get Tad to come down," and he did. And again, people went fucking nuts. And then it felt like he was in good shape.

DAVID GOTTLIEB: At some point in, I'd say March or April 2016, I was on the phone with Craig and he said, "Hey, you know, it's ten years of *Boys and Girls*, maybe we should do something, do some festivals." And I said, "Yeah, we can make that call, but there's no use doing it unless Franz is back in the band." "What do you mean?" I said, "Well, two reasons. One, he's all over that record. His creative stamp is in that record, and in those songs. Number two, when I talk to fans, it is usually the first thing they say to me: 'Is there any chance of Franz ever coming back?'" And Craig said, "Okay, give me a couple weeks."

CRAIG FINN: Gottlieb said we should do something for the tenth anniversary of *Boys and Girls in America*. I can't remember who it was who thought of going to the Brooklyn Bowl, but they were into it. And I think we went to Riot Fest, which often has a band playing a whole record. It just became obvious that if we were going to highlight *Boys and Girls in America*, we were going to need a piano player. Let's be honest with ourselves on that front: the first person we should call is the guy who played the piano.

FRANZ NICOLAY: I was surprised to see the name *Craig Finn* on my phone, because we hadn't spoken in literally six years, maybe a little longer. I let it go to voice mail and then I got the voice mail. I had expected something like that to happen. I had even told people when they asked, "Do you think you'll ever play with them again?" "Ah, there's going to be a ten-year *Boys and Girls in America* something. I bet it will come up." So it hadn't *not* crossed my mind.

CRAIG FINN: He either texted me or emailed me back. Rather than call me back. I was like, *Oh, that's not a good sign.*

FRANZ NICOLAY: I talked about it with my wife, and I said, "Fuck it," more or less. I had gone through a period in my life where I had decided that I was done playing music. I could make a living at the solo thing, but it wasn't setting the world on fire, and it required my playing hundreds of shows a year. I had kids and it became quickly clear that that was unsustainable. And so I went through a midlife-crisis period of a year and a half or so and then decided that I would try to close the door on that and turn to writing and teaching, which was right about the time that Craig called. Just when I thought I was out, they pulled me back in.

DAVID GOTTLIEB: About three weeks later, Craig called me back and said, "Okay, Franz is in." "Great, have you talked to everybody else?" "Yep." And so I think that was the beginning of Craig taking over shaping the direction. He's in the pilot seat. There had certainly been enough conversations between me and him, and between me and Tad, where I had repeated that democracy doesn't work. And a two-headed snake does not work. I don't know how Hall and Oates make it work.

FRANZ NICOLAY: There had been enough distance at that point where my profoundly mixed feelings had dissipated. Having gone through that process of deciding that I wasn't going to be a musician anymore, the stakes seemed lower. I had some anxiety about Steve, wondering, *Is this going to be one of these things where I've got to fight for space?* I was concerned that we would need to have a conversation about feelings. But that had never happened before, so why would it happen now? It definitely didn't happen.

BOBBY DRAKE: I was like, "Yes, please, get back in here." But he was probably a little reserved. He was my bunkmate: we've always gotten along.

TAD KUBLER: Franz was as blasé coming back into the band as Craig and I probably were about him leaving. It was bizarre. But I remember the first rehearsal, him showing up in a pair of jeans and a pair of Vans slip-ons, and I just thought, *What the fuck is going on here? Is this casual Friday? What happened?* But it was immediately good. I think over the course of the few years that he had left, I'd had plenty of time to be reminded of all the things that I'd loved about that guy, and when he came back, we'd all just grown up a little. He'd had kids, I wasn't getting loaded anymore, and our lives had started to happen outside of the band, which I think really helped put the band into better perspective.

STEVE SELVIDGE: I didn't know how it was going to play out. I didn't really know Franz that well; I never hung out with him. He was pretty quiet, he was a bit of an enigma to me. Still is sometimes. I had been covering keyboard parts, so I had to just undo a lot of muscle memory. But then I was like, *Oh God, I don't have to play that part anymore!* I just figured out the best way to make it the best that it could be. But I definitely wondered, *Okay, how's this going to go? Hope he's cool about it.*

CRAIG FINN: Steve and Franz, the way they've both found their place in this lineup is incredibly important to what's happened spiritually, musically, emotionally, whatever. They're both great musicians and great people, but they've actually hit it off on all fronts. And I think that that's really, really catapulted the band into new heights, musically, in the past few years. It's not lost on me that they're the two guys who largely lived out of town, they had kids roughly the same age, and they're very strong musicians, maybe the strongest within The Hold Steady.

GALEN POLIVKA: I was just hoping it worked on a short-term level. I was hoping the shows would be fun. I was hoping everyone would be in a cool place. We got up and running and writing new stuff pretty quickly. It didn't feel like a nostalgia act. It never felt like we were Kansas playing the state fair. I remember it being more fun than I thought it was gonna be and I was delighted that it was fun. It was like a vortex: everything disappeared into this black hole for seven years, and then you come out. I didn't know that we were gonna come out on the other side, even when the shows were booked. But it went super well, everyone showed up super prepared and super well-adjusted and ready to play music. We crawled out of the vortex or the abyss or whatever it was, and we were still a functioning thing.

DAVID GOTTLIEB: I think Tad was more open to it in the summer of 2016 than he would have been a year earlier. And I think it's because the silence of that one year of literally doing nothing was a reality check. Somebody's got to be the boss. I think Tad's own personal financial challenges played into it, because it was very easy to look at that and go, "You don't get to make

EXIT

the calls on the finances." And in 2016 we were sitting on this massive offer from the Brooklyn Bowl. And that's when the ideas for sound-check happy hour and advance merch bundles and all the various bells and whistles that we do came up. The one thing the band always said to me is, "One of the most important things to us is our relationship with our fans, and they're gonna be on you, and they're gonna be in your face, but they're the most important and we should always be doing things." And that stuck with me. And that actually opens up creative options.

CRAIG FINN: That first show at Riot Fest, we played the first few songs, and it was just like, *Oh, this is what we've been missing.* And that weekend went well. I remember saying to Franz, "Look, if we did these weekends at the Brooklyn Bowl, would you be open to it?" And he said, "Totally." We started slow, and kept adding them. But then when we actually played new recorded music, I think that was exciting for Franz, because there's a creative element to it and we could only go so long without adding that.

FRANZ NICOLAY: I remember saying when I left the band the first time that it was like I had died and I was reading my own obituaries. And then coming back, it was like, *He is raised, he has risen!* I thought a lot harder about it a year and a half later when Craig said, "Hey, do you want to think about writing some new songs?" It had been an emotionally difficult separation process. Having gotten through all that, it was like, *Do I really want to open that door again?* There was a reputational aspect of it: *People associate me with the best records that the band made, and if we try to make new songs and it's not good, do I want to open that door?* So I sort of tiptoed into it. Was it going to open up all these old creative conflicts that we used to have, in terms of everyone's different aesthetics?

TAD KUBLER: I can't remember if it was after the first year of Brooklyn Bowl in 2016, or even before we played those shows, but I said, "I really don't want to become like a heritage act," and I think Craig felt the same way. "We can't be doing RIP Fest next year just because the money's great. As long as there's some kind of creativity behind this, I think that'll help everything." But at that point, maybe it was just an idea.

DAVID GOTTLIEB: We did Riot Fest in Chicago, in Denver, and then went and played a festival in Toronto. Those three festivals were good first steps back into the pool. And they were easy because of *Boys and Girls*. It was clear from announcing the Brooklyn Bowl that we were on to something, because the tickets sold so fast. And that made the festival shows easy, because it gave everybody something to work on and be excited for: "Okay, these shows all went well and now we get to expand on that and do our own shows." And I think that first Bowl run felt better than anyone had anticipated, just from the fan reaction.

It wasn't long after that that the Empty Bottle in Chicago approached us about playing their twenty-fifth anniversary. Our response was, "Hey, we'd love to come play a show there. But for us to fly eight people there, your offer is just not there." And then we explained to them what we did with the Brooklyn Bowl. And they said, "We can do that. We'll pick a different venue. We'll pick a room in Chicago, we'll just do three nights and hit that thing."

We did that and we expanded on the fan events. We did a Q&A with a lot of fans. And that weekend in Chicago is actually the real beginning of The Hold Steady version 3.0. That weekend was so triumphant and so great, and I said to Craig, "We should do this every summer. We should call it 'Constructive Summer.' We should treat it like the NCAA basketball tournament and move it around." And he was like, "Yeah, that's a great idea. Let's work on that." And a couple of weeks later, he called me up and he said, "I'm just going to tell you: me, Tad, and Franz are working on a new song." That was around July 2017.

STEVE SELVIDGE: In 2017 we were playing three nights in Chicago and we decided—and this never really works as well as you would hope—to play covers by bands from Chicago. And so when we rounded the corner of really working on a Styx song, Finn said, "The amount of time we spent working up 'Too Much Time on My Hands' by Styx, we definitely, between four writers and everybody in the band, could come up with a song."

CRAIG FINN: We learned Wilco, "I'm the Man Who Loves You," and we learned Cheap Trick's "Southern Girls," then we learned the Styx song "Too Much Time on My Hands," and it ended up being a little bit challenging. I thought, *You know, we're trying to make something fun for the fans and do these kooky covers. What would be really more fun for the fans is if we dropped a new song.*

TAD KUBLER: It was tricky because it felt like Craig could come and go whenever he wanted, and the rest of us didn't have a lot of control over how the band would or could evolve. It was just going to be on those terms, and if that was a problem, then it was going to be a problem. But I think starting to work on new material was an indication that Craig was invested again.

CRAIG FINN: In our world, "Entitlement Crew" is a hit. It's a top-ten Hold Steady song from a fan's perspective. I knew that song was really special. Even just the opening—"*Tequila takeoff, Tecate landing*"—it's talking about drinking, it's Hold Steady. It felt like it captured something that I knew people were gonna like and that was exciting. By the time we played London [in March 2018], people were going fucking apeshit for that song. It was an immediate hit.

TAD KUBLER: In response to how dense stuff became on *Teeth Dreams*, and I can't re-

BY DOING MORE VULNERABLE SOLO RECORDS THAT FOCUSED ON SMALLER THINGS, I WAS EXCITED TO BE YELLING INTO A MICROPHONE ABOUT PEOPLE FUCKING UP

member if he suggested this or I did, but one of us said, "Why don't we go back to Lifter Puller? I'll start on bass, and we won't add any guitars until you've got the lyrics, so you know where it's going to sit and how it's going to fit in there, and then we can start to layer the guitars," and that's how we wrote "Entitlement Crew."

FRANZ NICOLAY: I've never talked to Craig about it, but my personal opinion is that "Entitlement Crew" was intended as a meta song to the fan base: *"Never got to say goodbye to you,"* and, *"Thanks for listening, thanks for understanding."* The band hadn't officially broken up; people had this unfinished feeling about it, I think: *Thanks for listening, thanks for understanding that we had to go through this period in the wilderness.*

CRAIG FINN: I thought we'd make kind of a real rough demo with Josh Kaufman—just me, Franz, and Tad—but once we got going, it just felt good, and I think more so than *Teeth Dreams* and *Heaven Is Whenever.* I felt like I'd gotten back to writing songs that felt like Hold Steady songs lyrically to me. I think part of it was that by doing more vulnerable solo records that focused on smaller things, I was excited to be yelling into a microphone about people fucking up.

JOSH KAUFMAN (PRODUCER, *THRASHING THRU THE PASSION* AND *OPEN DOOR POLICY*): I came in as "Craig's guy." One thing that immediately put me in good graces—though I was hard on them at first, because they were off a break and needed a boot camp—was that I could join in on how much we all looked up to and responded to Craig's writing. Even though I was his guy, and nervous about that, we were all on the same page in the studio: what sets us apart from every other band rocking in a bar is the mix of that with what Craig does lyrically. And Craig was excited

to have the guys back too. But there was a bit of anxiety from me. I was freaked out for the first few days because I felt they needed a bit more preproduction, and there we were burning up studio time.

FRANZ NICOLAY: It was baby steps every step of the way. The first recording session wasn't great, not through anyone's fault, but I think we didn't really know Josh, the band hadn't recorded in a long time, the comfort wasn't there. We got "Entitlement Crew" out of it, and a couple of the other songs, but it took a little while before we really felt like we were firing on all cylinders again.

CRAIG FINN: One of my things was, "We don't have a record deal, so the cool thing is, we know where our fans are, we have this great email list, we can just put something out." And I loved the idea of the quick turnaround to just put something out: there's no manufacturing, it's just like, "We've got a new song, we recorded it last week, here it is." So we were doing between four and six songs each time. That just felt like a good number to bite off. Usually that's two of Tad's, two of Franz's, one of Steve's. You could do that over a weekend or a couple-day period without settling in for a month to try to make this record. It takes some pressure off.

JOSH KAUFMAN: There was an effort to make the music a little more orchestrated. They had always used horns, but we got more ambitious with the horn arrangements. I'd never made a thrashy rock and roll record before meeting The Hold Steady, so I think there was a pairing of opposites that benefited both me and them creatively. I think they just trusted me. They trusted my musical sense to help shepherd their next phase of being a band.

CRAIG FINN: I kept saying we weren't going to put the songs into an album to keep the pressure off everyone. I was attracted to the idea of just putting them out digitally, straight to the fans. But it's strange, because so much of our listening is digital now, because no one takes it seriously unless it's an album. And I became aware of that. Josh also was like, "Okay, after *Thrashing*, the next thing we do is, we've got to make an album. You guys are gelling, and I think you can do something that's more considered as an album." I'm glad we did it too, because I do like writing an album, I like thinking about that many songs at once, you know, even if you're not writing them. You write ten songs over a period of time, but things reveal themselves to you and then you might lean into those things.

FRANZ NICOLAY: Nowadays, Craig puts out the bat signal, saying, "Hey, it's time to write some new songs," and Tad and Steve and I each cook up three to six demos apiece and put them in the Dropbox, and Craig sits with them and sees which ones he vibes with, and records a vocal, or learns them sort of on guitar and records a guitar/vocal demo of how he thinks the form should be. And then—I don't know if he does this with the other guys, he does it with me—I'll sort of recut the demo to that form and then he'll re-sing over that.

JOSH KAUFMAN: For *Open Door Policy,* it was only two sessions about six months apart. We were excited about cutting live off the floor because the band had got its sea legs back, so there was an energy. They were road-testing stuff again by that point and playing songs at their residencies. There was a focus on it being a record. There was more sitting back and thinking where the bread-crumb trails lead, how the songs fit together, how the stories echo in each other. There were things we paid attention to in a way we didn't so much on the first batch. Just from a production standpoint, it's hard for me to hear a group of songs that won't eventually be part of an album. So even on *Thrashing*—we have eight songs now, not released yet, what will these be? Well, eventually it will be an album. That's how lots of people make records now anyway.

STEVE SELVIDGE: I think he and D. James Goodwin brought depth to it by sometimes extracting stuff, by sometimes saying, "I know this is the way that you always do it, or this is the way you think you should do it, but let's try it *this* way." It's not always easy: it's sometimes frustrating. There's times where I'm just like, *What in the world are we doing?* but then the end product speaks for itself. But I think he has a playfulness and a light that really help with things, especially given that we had come back from a bummer narrative.

DAVID GOTTLIEB: I think Josh is probably the not-so-secret weapon. I think he is able to get a lot out of them in a short period of time. I think he speaks a language with Tad and Steve and Franz on the music-creation side that is able to prevent any friction in what's being constructed. And he's already got a relationship with Craig on the writing side, to be able to say, "Get rid of that line, come up with something else." There's a method to the way he works. They aren't goofing off when they go away for five or six days. One thing Craig said to me, "Oh my God, this was so much better than us booking a studio for a month and going somewhere." It forces the producer to work and not sit there and take a week to track drums. The band is all in the studio together doing their parts together. And nobody's leaving.

FRANZ NICOLAY: In the old days, I definitely felt like if I was trying to sneak something into a song that was a little outside the lines, that the way to do it was to reference a classic rock record that everyone knew and would be comfortable with. Those barriers aren't there anymore. Craig is really interested in whatever's a new sound now in a way that the band wasn't in the old days. Josh is really interested in that. I always thought that one of the real opportunities that The Hold Steady had was that Craig's thing is so distinctive, that you could literally put anything behind him and it's still going to sound like The Hold Steady because people are going to hear his voice and his distinctive lyrical sensibility and say, "Oh, yeah, that's The Hold Steady." And so the kind of musical background we can give Craig is literally limited only by what we feel comfortable putting behind him.

In the old days, if you brought something into the rehearsal studio that wasn't immediately legible to the rest of the band in terms of, "How are we going to play this?" that could be a hurdle to get over. Whereas now, you can present a fully formed arrangement and then, when the band plays it, it's going to sound like The Hold Steady. A lot of the demos for the songs on the last couple of records don't sound anything like they sound on the record, because once it's played by the six of us, it's going to sound like The Hold Steady.

CRAIG FINN: You should see my Twitter mentions. They are just filled with people who are all, *Oh, this sounds like a Hold Steady lyric!* And it's basically, *Blah, blah, blah, Minneapolis, blah, blah, blah, blah, blah, blah, something in Minneapolis.* There's only so much Mississippi River you can throw in there before it becomes a self-parody. But at the same time, I guess the fact that people are saying this sounds like me makes me think that I have a thing, which is pretty good. But I do sometimes roll my eyes: a sentence with the word *Minneapolis* to me does not sound like a Hold Steady lyric. But it cuts both ways. You're always trying to say, *Have I done that before?* That's something we constantly ask ourselves: *Did we already do this?* You know, because we're 125 songs into the band.

I felt like I was going to write myself into a corner if I stayed with the same characters. There's also just so many times you can rhyme *Charlemagne* with *he's in pain*. I think there's a lot more mental health parts to the newer records, and I think those things are connected. And that might be a connection you begin to see between the ages of thirty and fifty. *Wow, all this drinking, it isn't so fun anymore.* So I think that there's that, I think the characters have gotten a little bit older, I think that's been noted by other people. And I think I've become a better singer and I might write a little more toward that.

DAVID GOTTLIEB: My concern was: what do I have to do to avoid them repeating what had happened eight years previously? I didn't need to do anything. That appreciation for what

they had really rose to the top. They thought, *I'm forty-five years old. I'm still in a rock band. I have this other side to my life. But when I do the rock band, I have fun and I earn lunch.* And I want to emphasize the *have fun* part, because I think they're all having more fun now. They know how lucky they were to have The Hold Steady blow up when they were all in their early thirties. They know that's not the way it usually happens. And so I think they were all appreciative of getting this really unique second opportunity in their late forties.

CRAIG FINN: For me, a big part of this is just to keep working. That's really important to me; that's what I want to do. And if everyone said, "I don't want to do it," I think I would still, I would want to write as many songs as I do each year anyway, so I would want some outlet. But yeah, I think that there is a sense of, *Let's keep going.*

GALEN POLIVKA: The long and short of it is, it was just fun. I said to Tad that we should do this as long as it's fun. Now instead of actively avoiding everybody, we like to have dinner together. It's not *The Partridge Family.* We don't live together. But I went from not always enjoying everybody's company to enjoying everybody's company. And doing it intermittently is just easier on everybody's constitution and everybody's life outside of the band, and I think it does carry over to the art as well. The last two records I'm really proud of.

FRANZ NICOLAY: We're all happy to see each other now. We don't get sick of each other. We always have a project to be worked—either we're working on new songs, which is super exciting, recording, which is super exciting, or playing shows that everybody's going to be excited for, which is just exciting. We've sort of eliminated the parts that aren't fun, which I think is a cool place for a band in middle age to be, otherwise why would you do it?

STEVE SELVIDGE: We're all about to hit fifty or well into our fifties, so there's not a lot

WE'VE SORT OF ELIMINATED THE PARTS THAT AREN'T FUN, WHICH I THINK IS A COOL PLACE FOR A BAND IN MIDDLE AGE TO BE, OTHERWISE WHY WOULD YOU DO IT?

of room for bullshit or drama at this point. I enjoy writing, I enjoy the people, both in the band and the people around us. I feel like our band is somewhat unique in the way we operate and the people who are around us, and it was very much brought back home to me in London in 2022. To be able to go and see people . . . it's a community, and the barriers are blurred, and I like that.

CRAIG FINN: The camaraderie in the band is very fun. So is curating this music and creating a world that this music lives in, and having people thrilled by it, and taking part in it. The live thing is especially fun for me; I like the arc of the show, the way it lifts off. And I do like the travel. I mean, honestly, if it was me, I would play more. I think The Hold Steady is actually at the right level of how many shows we play. But I'd love to tour more on my own if the opportunity was there to make it work. One of the things in the pandemic I found I missed was not necessarily the show or the sound check, it was getting to the town a night early and having the beer in the hotel bar. You know, that sort of interstitial stuff that you don't think you're enjoying at the time so much but you really are.

TAD KUBLER: What do you say to somebody who asks, "What's the name of your band?" "We're The Hold Steady, we're one of the best live rock bands around." That sounds like a ridiculous thing to say. But after the last time we talked, I actually had to drive back to the city and I was going through Hold Steady songs. I listened to "The Swish," I listened to "Cattle and the Creeping Things"—by the way, "Barely Breathing" was sort of supposed to be "Cattle and the Creeping Things, Part 2"—I listened to "Oaks" from *Teeth Dreams,* and I listened to a bunch of songs from *Heaven Is Whenever,* and I just felt . . . *I can't believe that I have been part of that.*

TWELVE

WE ARE ALL THE HOLD STEADY

VOICES OF THE UNIFIED SCENE

I SANG TILL I WAS HOARSE, I DANCED, IT SEALED THE DEAL

In 2009, I had no idea how badly I needed to listen to The Hold Steady. In fact, I had no idea who they were. I was born in 1957 and my formative music years were in the '70s, graduating from the Beach Boys and country rock in high school to Bruce Springsteen and others when I was in college. I loved music, and it was a huge part of my life. Shows? I've seen Bruce about fifty times, the Dead more than a hundred, and the list goes on. Bootlegs? I still have the cassettes, thousands of them.

By the turn of the century, my ardor cooled; I became bored with what I was listening to. I just couldn't gather the energy or enthusiasm to listen to another artist's live rehash of old hits. Worse, I had stopped listening to music pretty much entirely. I love to listen to tunes in my car, but for a few years I rode around mostly in silence. I didn't know any newer artists. I was dead in the water.

But I had made a friend in the music world; his name is Peter Thompson and he's a schoolteacher from New Hampshire. We'd met online in Graham Parker's chat room and we became good friends. Peter is like an amateur A&R guy; he listens to tons of stuff, most of it quite obscure, and he started sending me CDs once or twice per year with stuff to listen to. It wasn't that I didn't like what he sent, but I'd listen to the CDs once or twice, and that was it. There was nothing that turned me on; nothing to break the doldrums. Until.

One night in early 2009, Peter sent me a link in an email with a one-line message that said, *Listen to this.* The link clicked through to The Hold Steady performing "Stuck Between Stations" on *Letterman*. I listened once, then again, and again. I played that clip at least thirty times in a row, with tears in my eyes. I could scarcely believe what I was listening to.

The next day I called Peter and asked him which album I should buy. I started with *Boys and Girls in America*, then *Stay Positive*. Come April, THS played in nearby Albany, New York, at a tiny upstairs club called Valentine's. I sang till I was hoarse, I danced, it sealed the deal. And there have been more than fifty more shows since. In May 2022, I celebrated my sixty-fifth birthday at the Horseshoe Tavern with the band that has kept me so very vital over this past decade. Only my first Bruce show in December of 1975 had that much of an effect on me.

I sometimes wish I was a music critic so I could express exactly why I have connected so closely

to the band's music. I do know I don't get tired of it, and I surely understand the lyrics and where the band is coming from. I know pretty much everyone who reads this will know what I'm talking about.

Over the last few years the Unified Scene has become part of my life, and I've made many good friends at the shows. I find that I connect effortlessly with other fans; I've never seen any altercations at a THS show, just a cohesive group of intelligent, kind, and like-minded individuals. There really IS so much joy!

-Bill Horton

THE HOLD STEADY CONTRIBUTES TO MY HIGHS AND LOWS

The Hold Steady is intergalactic. They carry me across emotional universes, haphazard relationships, the epochs of my youth and young adulthood.

An older man introduced to me to their music. That relationship is long gone; my love for the act remains.

I'm too serious. I studied THS lyrics religiously, amassing quotes almost to rival my collection of D.H. Lawrence and Edith Wharton. I still want *Damn right I'll rise again* inked on my lower back in Craig Finn's handwriting.

As a writer, most of my time with The Hold Steady was at home, through a screen, the stories and sounds filling my room so that I was less alone. The Hold Steady informed my writing, enhanced my dreams, and above all, dared me to live.

When my flight was delayed en route to a Hold Steady show, I bought another ticket to ensure I'd make the gig. I ended up at the Brooklyn Bowl early, squashed myself against the stage, and immediately made new friends. When Craig started up "Your Little Hoodrat Friend," I screamed.

Almost nothing beats that moment.

Everyone has a personal soundtrack of their lives. The Hold Steady contributes to my highs and lows.

The man who welcomed me to the Unified Scene was, unfortunately, abusive. We got into a Hold Steady show in Brighton, the night soon tarnished when I made the "mistake" of smiling at a man beside us, a man who smiled back, lit up by the light pouring off of the band we all loved.

I spent the rest of the night sulking by my jealous partner's side, when I should have done what The Hold Steady tells us all to do: dance it off!

THS writes songs about men and women struggling to make sense of their roles in the world. "How a Resurrection Really Feels" is the ode to my suicide attempt; "Your Little Hoodrat Friend" is simply "my song."

It's a joy and honor for this weird little alien to land on such a welcoming planet. There are others I'm glad to visit, even more frequently: My Chemical Romance's moody star (probably resembling Mars), or Rancid's grubby Milky Way. But no matter where I roam, The Hold Steady feels like home, and sounds like the independence I took so long to find, and in some ways am still looking for.

With so many dicks shooting into space, thank god we have one rock group who wants to make the journey fun.

–C.E. Hoffman

THEY COULD BE ASSHOLES

Don't meet your heroes, they say. That admonition was ringing in my ears on the flight from New York to Las Vegas in August of 2014. I have a long history of making impulsive, rash decisions based on what seems likely to be fun, especially if the fun in question has a musical flavor. So when presented with the opportunity to donate a decent sum of money to benefit

Jersey Mike Van Jura's kids, in exchange for the opportunity to jam with THS onstage somewhere, I bit. A few weeks later, the band's management presented me and the other jammers with a tour schedule and asked us to pick dates. NYC went quickly, and I was left with such marquee travel destinations as Akron, Boise, and Omaha. So I booked a weekend in Vegas.

The anxiety started immediately. How the fuck was this supposed to work? I didn't think I should roll in with a crew to sound check, disrupting what I know from experience can be a pretty fraught time for a road-weary band. My ride-or-die THS friend wasn't free that weekend, and my wife had to watch my little ones, so I'd be making the trip alone. I'm a pretty confident player, but even the E Street Band doesn't have all three guitars bashing away at the same time—so how was I going to fit in? And this was a one-shot take, so best not fuck up. And what amp am I plugging into? How's "Stations" going to sound with a Les Paul into a crystal-clean Jazz Chorus? Or (gulp!) a guitar going direct to the board?

And, most importantly, I had never met any of the boys in the band. They could be assholes.

I started hedging my bets.

First, I decided not to request to play on "Stations," as I assumed (rightly, it turns out) that every other weekend warrior was going to call for that one. So I picked "Hoodrat." To prep, I listened to recent live recordings, which was a very good thing, since Steve and Tad had made some rhythm adjustments from the studio recording. I opted to go in light—no camera, no pedals, and a guitar that isn't my favorite, in case Galen decided to go all "London Calling"/Prince on my ax. I made sure I had fresh strings and backups. I tuned and retuned obsessively. And at the designated unholy rock and roll hour of five p.m., I took a deep breath and opened the door to Vinyl, the venue at the Hard Rock, and interrupted sound check.

Introductions were made and small talk ensued. Galen and I figured out pretty quickly that we went to grade school together. A patch materialized, and I was plugged into Craig's amp, which, contrary to rumors on the rail, actually produces sound. Bobby counted off and . . .

I've played in bands most of my life—bar bands and college bands—with some truly accomplished musicians. But nothing prepared me for riding the tiger of a road-hardened, tight, straight-up r'n'r powerhouse. Even at sound checks with the thrusters at three-quarters, standing on the bridge of the THS rocket ship was face-melting. It felt like the whole band was creating a cresting wave, and then surfing it all the way to shore. Tad was worried I'd miss the changed rhythm cue, and was surprised when I nailed it. It was SO . . . MUCH . . . FUN! It ended too quickly for me, and probably not quickly enough for the band, especially since I hadn't factored in the breakdown. That's where Craig usually does his stream-of-consciousness ramble in the moment, which would have been very awkward during sound check in an empty room. Instead he let the three guitars fiddle around before the rocket blasted off again.

Everyone was so nice and supportive, from the band to the sound guys. I made an audio recording from across the room, and when I want to remember what playing in a world-class rock and roll band feels like, I'll put on the headphones and remember when.

I spent the show that night on the rail, shouting out lyrics along with another superfan, and got a nice little shout-out from Craig during the actual performance of "Hoodrat." When the show was over, I humble-bragged about my one-song stint with my favorite band, and obsessively repeated the most important thing I learned: they are not assholes.

-Rick Himes

I CRY DURING "KILLER PARTIES"

Every artist has its denomination of die-hard fans, and the die-hards have their own language: a private dialect of references and meta-references, in-jokes and obscure trivia, anecdotes and war stories traded like credentials. At Massive Nights each year, I get a kick out of observing its transmutation into the physical realm, which for Hold Steady fans amounts to a kind of DIY Olympic sport. I've seen countless tattoos, handmade back patches, and custom T-shirts, an ever-expanding roster of accessories in the shape of lyrical citations—party favors for the ultimate "if you know, you know" indie rock band.

Fittingly, for a band that draws from Kerouac as seamlessly as the punk rock pantheon, there's something both poetic and primordial about that language. After all, when we are signaling to each other our allegiance to The Hold Steady, what we are really acknowledging is how The Hold Steady signals to us: powerfully, profoundly, in beer-soaked bar-band sing-along songs that convey essential truths with the finesse of classic literature, the scope and pathos of myth. These symbols and slogans and tchotchkes, tiny little texts scratched or emblazoned, the bits of confetti I pick out of my clothes for weeks—their translation goes beyond a communal wink and nod. The root signal is one of intense, spiritual devotion.

I won't get it tattooed on my arm, and I'm not holding out hope for any officially licensed T-shirts, but maybe I should walk around with a placard this year. It would read, *I CRY DURING "KILLER PARTIES."*

Because you guys would get it: the self-deprecating humor, the abject sincerity, the fact that when I say, "I cry," I don't mean polite sniffles; I mean beer-drunk waterworks of pure and undiluted catharsis. You guys would understand that even though my weepy self-indulgence is totally ridic-

ulous, it's also something precious and sacred, an experience to be cherished. Every year, without fail, the song hits me like a freight train. I've heard it countless times, live and on record, and yet when the first weekend of December rolls around, it unfailingly obliterates me anew.

And each December, one of you sees me, and smiles knowingly, and sometimes even puts your arm around me.

I've spent sixteen years among the ranks of The Hold Steady die-hards—ages seventeen to thirty-three—which feels cosmically ordained for reasons I need not explain, because you all already know. And once upon a time, killer parties really did almost kill me. But when I hear that song each winter in New York, I'm not reflecting on those memories, or the many times that refrain has offered an acutely personal solace. I'm not looking backward at all. In fact, I'm barely looking inward. What I am experiencing is singularly current and radically present. It is a depth of feeling that only exists in the moment, in front of a stage, surrounded by other people who speak my language. I glance around and I am so rapturously happy to be right here, with all of you, right now, for the same reasons.

There is so much joy in that. How could I possibly contain it?

-Marisa Buxbaum

I ADDED A NEW VERB TO MY VOCABULARY

It's 2010, and my brother Alex and I drive from Georgia to Birmingham, Alabama, to see the rock show. We arrive early, so we decide to get front and center on the rail. We're close enough that we're standing over Craig's minimalist guitar board, a single tuner labeled, *Finn's Truth.*

After a perfectly pleasant opener and some college kids chanting "Roll Tide" during the break (it's no surprise they don't play the South much anymore), The Hold Steady takes the stage. It's the first interim six-man lineup, with Steve in Franz's spot and a keyboardist tucked way in the back, both on the stage and in the mix. The boys come out firing—the first four songs are the openers from the first four albums. The general-admission crowd is shoving their way to the front, as per usual. The people are packed in.

During "Stations," Alex and I notice a young woman behind us sobbing. They appear to be tears of joy. It's not uncommon to see someone shedding tears at these shows—I've done it once or twice myself—and they are soon overshadowed. Halfway through the song, I pick up an absolutely rancid stench. It's a fart, a bad one. I turn to Alex and mouth, *Did you?* He shakes his head and nods over to the woman. The song continues, and the smell keeps getting worse. By the time we all go down and drown in the Mississippi River, a three-foot perimeter has cleared out around her.

It looks like a bizarro version of the back cover of *Boys and Girls in America*, but instead of a boy and a girl standing alone on the dance floor, it's a girl and her gas. The odor dissipates, mercifully, and we all get along with the show.

I've now seen THS over sixty times, and so many shows have been special and uplifting. This little show wasn't particularly remarkable—it was a Sunday in Alabama, it was a transitional time for the band, Craig didn't tell a story during "Hoodrat," and the encore ended with "Stay Positive" instead of "Killer Parties." But it is still the only show where I added a new verb to my vocabulary: *cryfart*.

Alex and I still use it, and we can't see or smell one half of it without asking when the other half is coming. And whenever either of us is going through a truly emotional time, *cryfart* has given us a welcome bit of comic relief and a giggle when we really need it the most.

—Buddy Morrison

CRAIG REALLY NEEDS TO WORK ON HIS GOALKEEPING SKILLS

"We need at least two Gibson Hummingbird acoustic guitars." I already had to find a PA, a mixing board, and catering for 120 people, so the specificity of the request for the guitars threw me slightly.

Happily, my friend Richard owns about sixty guitars, including Gibson Hummingbirds. He said he would be delighted to have his guitars played by professional musicians, instead of him noodling on them.

I had only learned for definite that The Hold Steady was going to be able to play at my house in Leeds the day before the show. They were playing the Live at Leeds festival, and they had agreed to play my house during the day.

I told our guests that there were only three rules for the day. First, introduce yourself to anyone you don't know—we are all friends and fans, so kindness, mutual respect, and having a great time are paramount. Second, our home had two bathrooms, but with more than a hundred people crammed in, there was bound to be a line. Any American accents would almost certainly belong to band or crew, so guests were told to show them to the front of the line. Third, we would be raising money for the K&L Foundation, to benefit the family of the legendary THS fan Jersey Mike Van Jura.

Glad to say that everyone abided by those rules throughout. As Craig Finn later said about the day, "That was one for the ages."

Saturday, May 3, 2014, was warm and sunny in Leeds. It was my son Finn's ninth birthday, and he persuaded Craig to follow him on Instagram. That was despite my caution that Craig might then be inundated with pictures of Finn's pet rabbits. We had moved furniture from out of my sitting room via the French patio doors, into the garden, and set up the PA.

I later realized that having one's furniture in the back garden makes for a chilled-out vibe, whereas furniture in the front garden appears to make one a target for a muckraking TV documentary about people on welfare benefits. Who knew?

The band arrived and it was clear that they loved meeting all sorts of friends—old and new—outside the usual touring schedule of tour bus, hotel, venue. The gig itself passed by in a wonderful happy, confused blur, but some things stick in the mind. Craig had previously cautioned me about the perils of supporting the Minnesota Vikings. His warning had fallen on deaf ears, but did lead to a lyric change at the house gig on "You Can Make Him Like You"—*"If you get tired of his Vikings friends..."*

I saw Tad throw a napkin into a waste-paper basket, which he had scribbled on. I took it out of the bin—the napkin was the set list, which Craig and Tad had written a few minutes before they began playing. I still kick myself for not asking that "Banging Camp" be played, but it was important that the band did what they wanted to feel comfortable and as much at home as possible. That napkin is now framed and hangs on our living room wall.

While they waited for their tour bus to arrive, Bobby and Craig played football outside with Finn and Finn's friend Rohan. Finn vs. Finn in a penalty competition was something I'm very glad I saw. But Craig really needs to work on his goalkeeping skills.

I didn't realize until much later that Finn—my Finn, not Craig Finn—had stumbled over during the game. Bobby had helped him up, only for Finn to stand up quickly and crash his head into Bobby's face. That gave Bobby a black eye so bad that he struggled to see out of it onstage that night. If you look carefully at some of the band's publicity shots taken later that week for *Teeth Dreams*, the black eye was still visible.

I know that you can only blame the parents, and I'm very sorry.

I'm not sorry, though, for the memories from a unique day where everything great about the band and the community around it was on vivid display.

-Howard Roberts

HOWARD'S GENEROSITY AND KINDNESS CAME AT A TIME WHEN I NEEDED THEM

One of the greatest things about The Hold Steady is the community you become part of if you're a fan of the band.

I was having a tough time in 2014. I'd been working far too hard in a place that cared little for the impact certain things had on the people it worked with or for. THS played the Bush Hall, London, on a Sunday in May, and aside from the Manics' *Holy Bible* gigs, there's no other gig that I wanted to go to more that year. Alas, I couldn't get a ticket.

I went on the Unified Scene forum on the afternoon of the gig on the off chance that someone had a spare ticket, and someone did. Lots of Unified Scene members will know or know *of* Howard Roberts; I haven't seen him since, but will forever be grateful to him for that day. Howard met me outside the venue, refused to take any payment for the ticket, took me to the bar, and asked for assistance as he bought drinks for every member of the forum who was at the gig, and shepherded me down to the front couple of rows, where he'd been before coming outside to meet me. He seemed surprised but delighted that I liked The Hold Steady so much and had been to see them a number of times before, and we had a great chat about how we got into the band before they came onstage and started with "I Hope This Whole Thing Didn't Frighten You," the song I wanted to see most.

That gig came at a time that I really needed to be at a Hold Steady gig, and, though I didn't realize it before, Howard's generosity and kindness came at a time when I needed them too. It is, in my view, a wonderful instance of the brilliance of the band and their fans.

-Vicky Ward

THERE IS SOME AMOUNT OF BRAVERY IN SHOWING LOVE

I've never really been a kid at a Hold Steady show. I'm Craig's age. I grew up in the St. Paul suburbs; he grew up in the Minneapolis suburbs. We were at a lot of the same shows, we've figured out over the years, though he no doubt went to more. We probably bumped shoulders at Let It Be Records or Northern Lights. I know he was at a Green Day in-store at the record store I was running in around 1991.

My first rock show in a club was the Suburbs at First Avenue in the late '80s, the first of a number of the band's "farewell" shows. (That "farewell" thing never stuck; they're still going strong today.)

After years of seeing kids' music in connection with our radio show (*Spare the Rock, Spoil the Child*), our daughter Ella's first "grown-up" rock show in a club was none other than The Hold Steady at the tiny Iron Horse in Northampton, Massachusetts; she's continued to see the band regularly, including coming down for the final night of Massive Nights every year while she was in college. Our son Liam's first visit to First Avenue's main room was the band celebrating the venue's fiftieth year (a couple of years late; thanks, COVID)—and his first visit to the 7th Street Entry was the band there the next day. Not long after, he declared a music major. Probably not related, but you never know.

For all three of us, those early shows are almost unfair to all the other bands in the world yet to be seen. But the shows have also planted the seeds for what promises to be lifetimes of supporting live music. Last night, Liam (now in college) texted us video of a local band, Scrunchies, covering a Breeders song at the Entry. Ella (in grad school in Chicago) went on a spur-of-the-moment road trip to see Ezra Furman in Indianapolis—and Ella's first Furman show was when she opened for The Hold Steady in Brooklyn.

It is one of the touchpoints of every show that Craig declares, "There is so much joy in what we do up here," and it's worth paying attention to it as not just a part of the ritual. It might not get enough attention that this phrase is not just descriptive, but also prescriptive. It's telling everyone that shows should be joyous occasions, that being able to come together and close up the gaps between us—to borrow a phrase from Frank Turner—is something not to be taken for granted.

I'm writing this a couple of weeks out from being part of a memorial service for my friend Jon, a music lover who died suddenly, just a few years older than I am. The last time I saw Jon was at the Green River Festival—a stage and a PA in western Massachusetts. In putting together what I'm

saying at the service, I've been listening to music by a different Minnesotan named Craig—Cloud Cult's Craig Minowa. In one song, Minowa talks about what gets measured at the end of one's life: *"They'll measure up your heart to see / how much love you kept buried and how much love you were brave enough to show."*

It occurs to me that there is some amount of bravery in showing love (and joy) in the often-cynical world of rock music in the twenty-first century. Maybe that's what puts The Hold Steady shows in a different category from a lot of what's out there, and why so many of us make those treks to the shows.

The joy isn't just up on the stage, at least not on most nights. That's because we are all—we are *all*—The Hold Steady. Including the kids.

-Bill Childs

I'D NEVER BEEN HAPPIER TO HAVE SOMEONE NOT BE IN LOVE WITH ME

I first heard *Boys and Girls in America* driving to the wedding of the woman whom I once thought I would marry. I arrived in town three hours early and I was nervous about running into the family and friends of the bride-to-be: the last time I had seen any of them had been when they also thought I'd be the groom. I deployed a move I've perfected over years of being annoyingly early to everything: I drove around aimlessly, hoping to get lost enough that by the time I recovered, I'd be on time (or fashionably late). I had made a playlist of different albums, starting with *Boys and Girls*—a friend recommended the album to me because they knew I liked songs "where things happen" and I always like to listen to something new when I have a long drive. When I reached the end of the album, I broke the rules of the "long-drive playlist" and I started it over; I was not ready to leave this album just yet, because there was no more perfect soundtrack to my day. These people wanted to belong, but didn't; they needed to fit in, but couldn't; most importantly, they were too stuck in the promise of their own past to acknowledge that their future needed to be something completely different.

As I drove up and down the main roads of the small Massachusetts Cape town, I replayed "Party Pit" at least ten times. The repeated *"Gonna walk around / Gonna walk around / Gonna walk around and drink"* served as the perfect parallel to my aimless wandering, not just on that day but for the years leading up to it. By the fourth listen through the album, I felt like I'd unlocked something that had been trapped. Without realizing it, I'd been holding onto a vague hope of a "do-over," as lacking in self-awareness as Charlemagne, Holly, and everyone else who buried themselves in massive nights to avoid confronting complex days. These were my people.

When I made it to the wedding, for the first time I was able to see my friend as the person she'd

become, rather than who she'd been to me years ago. I'd never been happier to have someone *not* be in love with me. For me, *Boys and Girls in America* revealed that it was time to stop trying to hold onto the person I thought I was supposed to be and start looking for the person I'd become.

–Tim Howd

I STILL FEEL THAT HUG

In December 2013, my sister-in-law was admitted to a hospital in Albany, New York. She was thirty-three, had run her first 5K a couple of weeks earlier, and suddenly couldn't catch her breath walking up a flight of stairs. A trip to urgent care was followed by an emergency ambulance ride. Three days later she was scheduled for an emergency operation: she had a particularly aggressive form of kidney cancer.

I had known Danielle since she was the thirteen-year-old little sister to the woman I would later marry. She was the baby sister I never had.

When we got the call, we jumped in a car in the middle of a huge snowstorm and drove from Jersey City to Albany to be with her. We'd stay in a hotel for almost two weeks.

As Danielle recovered from the surgery, our entire family took turns sitting with her telling her stories, laughing with her, and listening to the things she wanted to do when she was back on her feet. On my turns, we'd close our eyes and I would narrate the hikes we were going to take together.

One afternoon, I was sitting with Danielle during an especially hard day. We talked about how she needed to stay positive if she was going to get through this. I played "Stay Positive" for her, and we sang along to the *"woah woah woahs."* It was her first time hearing The Hold Steady, and that sing-along song became our scripture. Whenever she was down, we'd sing it and smile to each other. Before too long, she was back on her feet and recovering.

In February 2014, I got the email: in April, The Hold Steady would be playing a small bar in Albany called the Hollow. We both knew we needed to go to that show, and we needed to hear that song. The main set concluded. We didn't hear "Stay Positive," but it didn't matter. We hugged and waited for the band to come back onstage.

Deep into the encore, the second-to-last song of the night, we heard it: *"I've got a lot of old friends that're getting back in touch . . ."* I put my arms around my baby sister. We hugged. We screamed the *"woah woah woahs."* And we cried. A lot.

Danielle's disease came back, and she passed away almost two years later. While I'm no longer married to her sister, I still feel her loss. But I also still feel that hug, and I still feel the joy we had together singing along to that song. And I still get a tear in my eye when I see it live.

-Damien LaVera

LET'S GET MORE LADIES TO THESE SHOWS

I fell in love with The Hold Steady when I heard "You Can Make Him Like You" in 2006, and it's been carrying me ever since. To dozens of shows, with thousands of people, through some of the happiest moments of my life. I am also a mother of two, a wife, and a lawyer who sometimes looks around and doesn't see very many people living the type of life I want to live. But every time I think about a girl who doesn't *"have to go to the right kind of schools"* but can let her *"boyfriend come from the right kind of schools,"* I am reminded that sometimes you can be your own role model and find inspiration in unexpected places. There is so much joy in that. Now let's get more ladies to these shows!

My sister and I used to work at the 9:30 Club in Washington, DC, and she got married during the pandemic. When I realized we weren't going to be able to throw her a bachelorette party, I asked the former GM if we could rent the club for a night. A few hundred dollars, an LD, a big stage, and six girls—I have never had a better time. And of course I took the opportunity to sing this song at the top of my lungs—although watching the footage, I realize I unfortunately have some work to do on my performance.

Side note: I asked my husband to start playing *Almost Killed Me* when I went into labor with my first child, and the baby was born before we got to *Separation Sunday*. It's my only regret.

-Sharon Desh

I FELL IN LOVE INSTANTLY

I was introduced to THS in a special way. My beloved friend Tim LaFollette was doing some video production/editing work for the band around the time *Boys and Girls in America* dropped. This was before he was diagnosed with ALS. He sat me down in excitement to make me listen to the album in a house that is not fifty yards from the house I live in today in Greensboro, North Carolina. I fell in love instantly. There's no doubt that his love for the band and this record contributed to that. We lost Tim to ALS in August 2011 at the age of thirty-one. He was such a rad person and I will always carry this memory of him every time hear "Stuck Between Stations" cranked up through to "Southtown Girls." I feel him right there with me as I look down the street at the house where he played it for me on that first night. I am doing that right now while writing this, overwhelmed with emotion. A special memory for a special album from a special band.

-Michael Sileno

MY DAUGHTER ASKED A SIMPLE QUESTION

My introduction to The Hold Steady came about three years ago when my then-three-year-old daughter asked if there were any songs with her name in them. So I punched *Esther* into Spotify and clicked on the first tune—and inside ten seconds, I was hooked. I plunged into the back catalog and very quickly became caught up in the wonderful tales of THS lore. A new favorite band with so much music, only discovered through my daughter asking a simple question! And I still regularly get asked to put on "Esther in the Kitchen" for her.

-Craig Collins

WAS PAUL NEWMAN IN THE HOUSE?

In October of 2006 I was put on a new medication that severely dried out my skin. With that came dandruff, and with dandruff came googling-for-a-cure. What I landed on was apple cider vinegar. Soak my head in it, get the pH of my skin back in balance, and I'd be in business.

On October 26, 2006, my new favorite band played my favorite venue here in Chicago, the Metro. They had just played Lollapalooza and impressed me and everyone I was with. But everyone was busy on the twenty-sixth, so I had to make the decision to go to my first concert by myself or miss what felt like might be a legendary show. I made the right decision, and I had some plans all to myself that night.

So on went my nightly dose of vinegar, followed by my Local H shirt, my concert shoes, my hoodie, and off to the train I went. All was fine on the trek to the train, the train ride, the walk to the Metro, in line at the bar, and weaving through the crowd to catch some Sean Na Na. It was warm in the Metro, especially in my hoodie, and I started to sweat. I was enjoying the music but kept getting distracted by an odor. Was there an all-you-can-eat salad bar nearby? I didn't put two and two together, and others seemed to be looking around wondering where the smell was coming from as well. Was Paul Newman in the house?

Then it hit me—it was *me*. Should I turn around, head home, and pretend this never happened? Would everyone be the oil to my vinegar and start to separate from me, singling me out? A couple of songs passed, and a group of women in front of me kept turning around, obviously to solve the mystery of the smell. I overheard one girl saying she had driven in from Minnesota for the show, and then she turned around to talk to me—10,000 lakes meets 1,000 islands.

But we didn't talk about salad, or lettuce, or interesting smells. She asked if it was the first time I had seen The Hold Steady, explained she was in town celebrating her friend's birthday. She could tell I was there by myself and let me know I was welcome to hang out with her and her friends. A

few minutes later, the guitar for "Stuck Between Stations" kicked in, and 1,099 others started feeling the joy that I instantly felt. I might have gone to the show by myself, but I definitely wasn't alone.

–Anthony Stephens

THE MUSIC NEVER STOPS MEANING SOMETHING

I wasn't there in 2003 when The Hold Steady played their first ever show, at Northsix, but I did see my first Hold Steady show there in the winter of 2005 or 2006. I drove down from Providence and stayed with my brother. We went with some of his music-writer friends—I'd ordered a ticket online, and felt embarrassingly provincial about it as they entered empty-handed, giving their names at the door. Someone bought me my first-ever Four Loko and I took about two sips before gagging on the cough-medicine taste and handing it off to a stranger. After that, I bought myself a normal beer. I don't remember the particulars of the set list, but it pretty much had to be songs off their first two records. I remember screaming along and spilling out onto the street at the end of the night, hoarse and joyful and sweaty and buzzed, giddy at the prospect of moving to New York after I graduated that spring.

I had first heard "Your Little Hoodrat Friend" on a compilation CD that had come polybagged with an issue of *Jane* magazine, and it so electrified me that I'd bought *Separation Sunday* the next day. A week later, I went back for *Almost Killed Me*, and I would have listened to those albums exclusively through my senior year of college if my roommates hadn't insisted I switch it up sometimes.

Later, I'd work as an assistant at a magazine owned by the same company that published *Jane,* and it thrilled me to ride the elevator with their editors, though by then, Jane herself was gone and so were many of the people I'd admired in those pages. A year or two after *Jane* folded, I became an editor for the other magazine's website, and I remember sitting through a meeting with the consumer-marketing department while they explained why these flimsy messenger bags would make the best gift for new subscribers. They said athletic socks were also a good option. After the meeting, I went to Bryant Park and cried. Those piece-of-shit bags would never mean anything to someone, and neither would my work.

Just after that, The Hold Steady played their tenth-anniversary shows at Music Hall of Williamsburg—the former Northsix. I got a little self-conscious about screaming along and head-banging and doing the things you generally do when you're in a sold-out room with loud guitars—I was never as punk as I wanted to be and I got less punk as I got older. I'd been making a concerted effort to resist nostalgia, but I still got sentimental about the other Hold Steady shows I'd been to since college, and about the many, many moments in my life their music has been the soundtrack to.

Mostly, though, what I thought about was how loving something can fill you with so much joy. I heard a song when I was twenty-one and it unlocked a room in my tiny heart and shined light into it, and all these years later my life looks a lot different but that room is still there and the song is still the key. Standing there next to my brother—like we did at my first show, and also not at all like that—I felt a surge of gratitude to him and to *Jane* and to The Hold Steady and to all the threads that connect the person I am now to the person I was then. How lucky I am that the music means something to me, that it never stops meaning something, that it never stops meaning something different.

-Ruthie Baron

(A version of this essay was originally published on Tumblr in 2014.)

I FELL BACK IN LOVE WITH MINNEAPOLIS

The summer my marriage broke up was the year "Constructive Summer" came out. I spent months driving between Milwaukee and Minneapolis job hunting, trying to find a place to live, and figuring out how to live with my daughter in another state. On one of my drives I heard this new station named the Current and Barb Abney asking for a top-three playlist. My daughter was maybe three years old and she and I had an "Inny-Minnie-Apolis" playlist and it featured "Party Pit" (she is seventeen now and we still visit the Grain Belt Bridge in bright, new Minneapolis when she is in town). I sent three songs from the list to Barb Abney and three days later I heard my name and my three favorite Hold Steady songs. I knew at that moment life was going to work out, and I embraced the change and fell back in love with my life and Minneapolis.

-H.J. Gillham

CRAIG GOT LOCKED IN THE TOUR-BUS TOILET

It must have been a weekend in the summer of 2007. I was blissfully unaware of The Hold Steady and I was in my local HMV record store in Belfast, Northern Ireland, browsing the CDs. The dudes behind the counter looked like a pair of refugees from the Allman Brothers Band and they were choosing the tunes that played across the store. Then they put on *Separation Sunday* and I was transfixed. I'd never heard anything so lyrically dense that still rocked: it hit me hard. I remember that the line to the cash register was really long and I had a chance to listen to

a few songs before I brought my purchases up to one of the Allmans. As he was ringing them up, I asked, "Who's that playing?" and that's where I first heard of The Hold Steady.

We chatted for a bit (which explained why the queue was so long and slow-moving) and the guy raved to me about how great this band was. I muttered that I'd consider buying the album but I wasn't going to endure that queue again, so the cashier darted off and got me a copy. Just as I was leaving, he said, "See you next week!" I was puzzled—there was something in his tone that implied that it was more than a casual shopper/cashier exchange. I must have looked as quizzical as I felt, and he explained: "I think you'll be back next weekend to buy some of their other albums." He was wrong. I was actually back the following Wednesday and bought *Almost Killed Me*. A week later I completed the set with *Boys and Girls in America*.

I've only gotten to see The Hold Steady play once—at the Limelight in Belfast. The show started late because Craig had gotten locked in the tour-bus toilet and it ended early because the bar wanted to do a quiz night or something equally banal. I may not be a superfan in having attended many shows, but I did have to convince a doctor to check me out of a hospital early to attend the gig—I'd been in for surgery and had to stay a couple of nights to recover. I was just about mobile, and still with stitches in, but I wasn't going to miss that night.

-Robert Chapple

HUMANS ARE CONDUCTORS

It was a summer in which everything we built kept more out than it kept in. Restless, anxious, and soundless, we trudged into the first winter of quarantine. It acted much the same as the summer and spring before that, looking out our windows at the world passing by, the miasma of COVID hanging over us like a guillotine to a good time. I hadn't seen a show since February, and to call it an itch is an understatement to the ways I wished to scratch. The Hold Steady announced they were pressing on with their annual Massive Nights with a salient twist: the shows were to be a completely virtual event. I couldn't buy tickets fast enough.

On the night, I cozied up in bed with my cat Lugosi and my laptop, the device which had been my medium in teaching fourth graders for the past eight months (may we never have to do that again). As the window opened, and feedback started to pour out of my speakers, I got emotional. I truly felt I was *with* Craig Finn and Co. Seeing the arrays of screens with people all around dancing, drinking, singing along, I began to believe that what we built maybe wasn't entirely a Jericho.

So, of course, as the hits kept rolling, we started our march. The poster on my wall from that night reads, *Streaming from Brooklyn to your living room with 100,000 watts of power.* I tell my students that humans are an example of a conductor. I watch on the screen as people in other living rooms cut the rug for no one in particular and everyone by desire. In this way, by the jolt of electric rhythm, anchored by one sonic pulse, we are truly unified.

-JR Rhine

"Hey, I know you," said the tall blonde in the Hampton Inn lobby.

I'd flown from Philly to Tampa in January to see a band in sketchy Ybor City. Maybe it was a midlife crisis, but certainly not all of us were in crisis. Somehow a band had taken so much of what I loved—music, lyrics, shows—and transformed it into what I needed. And, yes, I knew the blonde and she knew me; we were friends from an Internet message board, though we had never met in person.

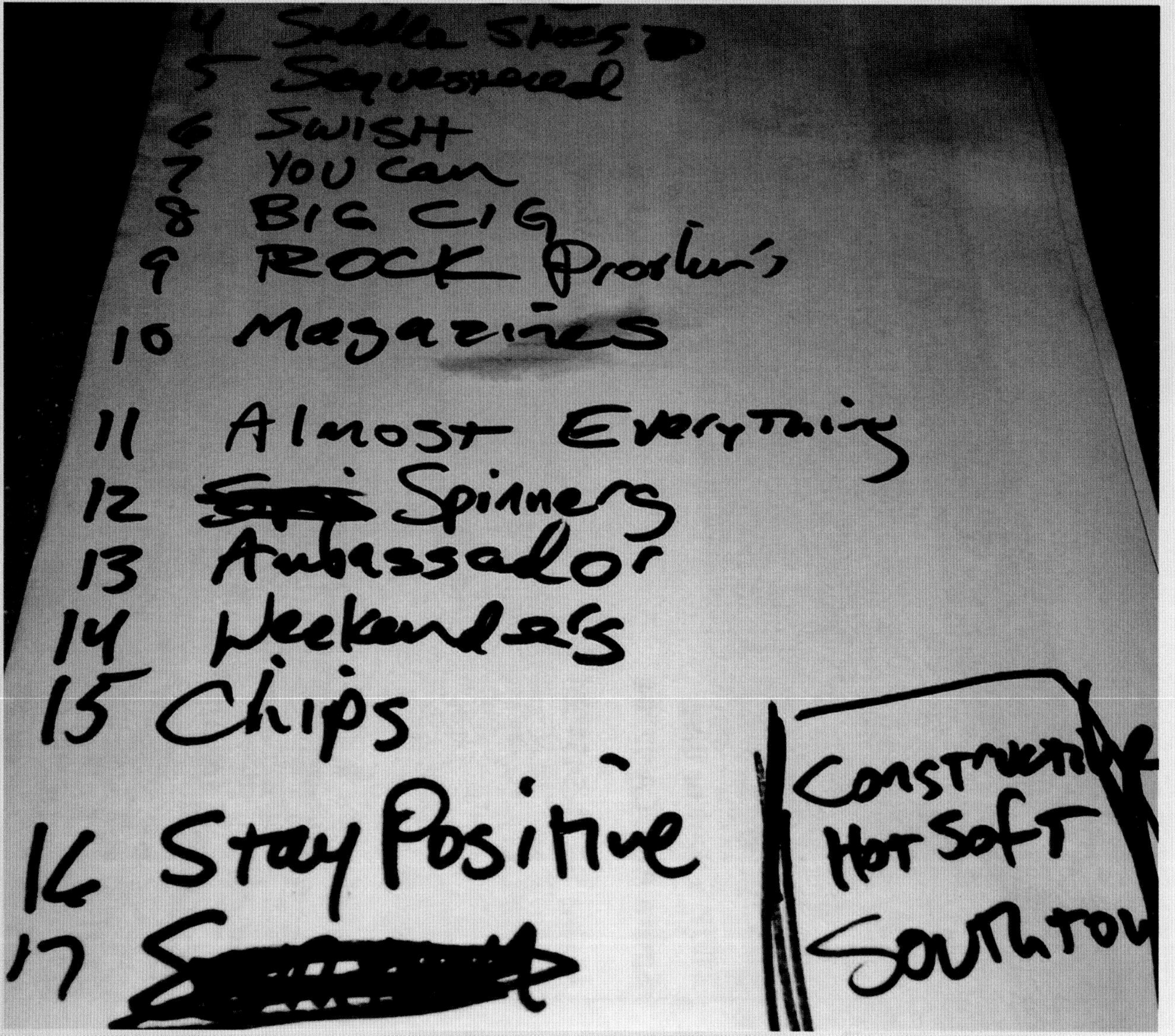

I first heard The Hold Steady after NPR's *All Songs Considered* praised *Boys and Girls in America*; it was love at first listen. The band hit my rock and roll sweet spot—funny, dark, abundant lyrics delivered by a unique voice against a riff-laden soundtrack. I discovered and lurked on their fan message board where members told their own, often personal stories. I eventually joined them, picking a screen name that playfully tweaked some of the New York baseball fans on the board—*Phils_fan.*

I felt vulnerable when I started writing but was welcomed like a long-lost friend. The board was populated with smart, literate people who loved thinking and talking about music. We grew to know about each other—our lives, our families, our jobs (it only seems like 71 percent of Hold Steady fans are lawyers).

The Ybor City show was our pilgrimage. The band sang about it and we needed to get together there to celebrate. We met in hotel lobbies, drank in pool halls, and hugged onstage with the band at the end of the show. Technology brought us together, but it was the shows that unified us. Friendships that were born anonymously online were consecrated in a haze of beer, Jell-O shots, eight ball, and real names and faces.

My wife and I visited NYC a half dozen times that year to see shows with our new friends and many message-board denizens who hadn't made it to Ybor City. We bought each other T-shirts, tickets, cab rides, and drinks. I've traveled to three countries and many states to see the band and knew people at every stop. Fellow fans contacted me when they visited Philadelphia to get together even when there wasn't a show in town, making me feel like an ambassador for my hometown.

Through the band and Unified Scene, I've attended weddings and known people who died (RIP Mike, Mark, and Liz). The kids at the shows had kids of their own. Many of us are off the message board now, but we still send postcards, photos, and texts. As Craig Finn says at the end of every show, "We are all The Hold Steady." Happy anniversary to all of us.

-Neil Margolis

MY KIDS WERE UNIMPRESSED

My story takes place in summer 2018. I live in a small-market town in the UK. I've never drunk alcohol, never smoked, never taken drugs, so as a fan I'm probably an outlier. My two children, as children do, have grown up considering my life as a base level of normality, perhaps a little too suspicious of more alternate lifestyles and people.

I realized it would be a great lesson for them if their father embraced something unexpected. I wasn't about to start drinking or smoking, and as a middle-aged man in a small town, I wouldn't know where to get drugs. There was only one option—get a tattoo. But what tattoo? No question, the *Stay Positive* logo was an obvious choice. Without wanting to sound like a Zen-lite airhead from a song like "The Prior Procedure," *Stay Positive* as an ethos, and as an album, means a lot to me. I believe we sometimes have to make a deliberate decision to stay positive. The world can be a hard place at times, with all the famine and death and pestilence and war. It's easy to only see the negatives, not the benefits. Staying positive isn't always easy, but it brings its own rewards. Also, I'd seen the band raise the roof at the Lexington in London that March, so it would be a double reminder of what The Hold Steady means to me.

I tried a couple of tattoo parlors in town, both booked up, then found one that could do it there and then. In retrospect, that should have been a warning sign. Eager to get it done, I committed. My main memory is that it hurt. A lot. So much more than I expected. It's only a small tattoo on my upper arm, a couple inches long, not a major piece of ink by any means, but by god it was painful. After it was done, I walked home feeling kind of cool and also wondering when my arm would stop hurting. My kids were unimpressed.

In truth, my tattoo isn't very good. The ends of the top and bottom curves go too near the plus sign in the middle, so from a distance it looks like a figure eight, not the *Stay Positive* logo. If I was having it done again, I'd just have the outlines done, not have it filled in. Often I barely remember it's there, then I'll catch sight of it in the shower and remember an amazing night at the Lexington, a failed attempt to widen my kids' perspective, and a reminder to stay positive.

-Michael Hudson

THE HOLD STEADY GUIDED ME HOME

I first heard of The Hold Steady from a poorly copied, paisley-blue flyer tacked to the dining hall's message board for a show they were doing at the University of Minnesota. My friend was a volunteer at the event—"Lend a Hand, Hear the Band"—and offered to add me to the guest list. I can't remember what song they played for me, but whatever it was, it didn't spark anything in me then. But they still gave me their extra ticket in case I changed my mind. I didn't.

The following fall, I transferred to a university in Indiana, several hundred miles away. Surrounded by cornfields and one-stop-sign towns, I began to miss the Twin Cities, which I had only begun to explore shortly before I left.

I can't remember exactly how I found my way back to The Hold Steady—maybe it was from a post on someone's Tumblr or from a Last.fm recommendation—but I do remember what finally lit that spark: Finn's dense, knotted yarns about the cities I loved and missed.

This was back before you could easily stream music online, so I listened to what I could on YouTube, but mostly I read and reread Finn's lyrics on Genius. They became an oral history of a home I had left behind; an organic geography that lived and breathed between beers and hard-liquor chasers; nostalgic vignettes of a life I had half lived—the part-time job at Target in the Quarry next

to the Party City; my daily commute across the bridge where John Berryman tried to fly; the sly wink of the Grain Belt Bridge seen from bus windows.

My slow journey back across the Midwest took years and suffered several false starts, but all the while, The Hold Steady kept me connected to the Twin Cities. When I was finally able to move back, it was like meeting an old friend again as I rediscovered the streets and neighborhoods that had sung a chorus through my speakers. I was home and The Hold Steady guided me there.

-Ethan Merrick

THE UNIFIED SCENE HAS MADE ME A BETTER PERSON

We live in a society that strives for equality, diversity, and acceptance. We try to produce a society where no one is looked down upon because of their race, religion (or lack of one), nationality, age, skin color, creed, gender, sexuality, disability, body shape, accent, etc. All these things we strive for. To eliminate discrimination in any form. To make a classless society a reality. But has society achieved this? Probably not. Not completely anyways.

There's one place that it is achieved, however: the Unified Scene. Here, no one is judged by others; everyone is accepted. Everyone is friendly. Everyone is a brother or a sister. There's an unspoken code that is pretty much adhered to everywhere the Unified Scene gathers, especially London and New York. It's not achieved by mandates or laws or instructions being thrown around. It's achieved by self-policing and respect. When Craig says, "WE ARE ALL," never have such simple words been so profound.

The Unified Scene has made me a better person. More patient, warmer. Less grumpy. I've done things that have surprised myself. Opened up my home to other fans coming to gigs, people who in the real world live under real-world rules I don't really know that well. There's no cliques among the Unified Scene; there's old friends for sure, but I've never been to a single gig without making at least one new friend.

On March 13, 2021, I suffered a heart attack. After being told that during the emergency procedure at the hospital I had passed to the other side for twenty-five or thirty seconds, I remember my first thoughts were of my beautiful wife and best friend (and just as much of a fan as me) Theresa. The next thought was being thankful that I hadn't seen The Hold Steady for the last time. That's how much they mean to me—the band and the scene.

In December 2021, I felt strong enough to go to Massive Nights in Brooklyn. Dave Gottlieb organized a seat for me as I wasn't up to the rough-and-tumble of the pit. Another example of the special atmosphere around the band. After a slow rehab, I was unsure of how I'd be able to go, to be honest, but the kindness shown to me by Unified Scene members was beyond touching.

That is how a resurrection really feels.

-Bill Anderson

I LOVED YOUR STORY—MY SON IS IN A BAND!

In January 2005, I was looking to expand my life just a little bit, and figured a storytelling class would be a good diversion from my tech job. A noncredit night session through the local university, taught by local actor/monologuist John McGivern, seemed perfect. I showed up to the first class and noticed that the students skewed, well, older. I learned that retired public school teachers could take any of the classes for free, so they tended to fill up the courses. I got to know them well: it was mostly ladies my mom's age, who were the life of the class and had no shortage of stories. Judy, Sharon, Betty, Faye—if John was Milwaukee's answer to David Sedaris, then these were our Golden Girls.

Even though it was very clear that getting up in front of a group to talk was core to the class, there were few volunteers most nights. John would give us prompts to develop short spoken stories, and one evening he wanted to hear about times we just put ourselves out there, times we made ourselves uncomfortable in front of a crowd. I raised my hand and told a quick story about the rock band my friends and I formed in college—how Radioactive Sludge consisted of four guys who could not keep time and could barely play our instruments, but managed to talk our way into opening for a band at a local dive bar.

After class, Faye rushed up to me and said excitedly, "I loved your story about being in a band, because my son is in a band! He was in Milwaukee, then went to Minneapolis, now he's in New York. He plays bass—here, look at this!" Then Faye Polivka, Galen's mother, reached into her purse and gave me photocopies of their press clippings. They had gotten early buzz in *Rolling Stone* and *Spin*, and she couldn't have been more proud.

That's how I was introduced to The Hold Steady—by a retired schoolteacher and one-woman amateur PR agency. I immediately got *Almost Killed Me* and fell in love with the band and their sound. My first time seeing them live was with Faye as well. She let us know the band was playing at a Milwaukee bar, so we had a small reunion shortly after our storytelling class ended. Faye got a special shout-out from Craig and the guys—they were all crashing at her house that night.

–Tom Martin

THE FIRST PLACE I EVER REALLY FELT LIKE I COULD BE MYSELF WAS IN THE CROWD AT A HOLD STEADY SHOW

"K*alamazoo, we came here to tell you the truth. And the truth is, you can make him like you."* Craig said those words the second time I saw The Hold Steady. He had probably said it before and he has definitely said it since, but it was this time that I heard it.

I was at the show, alone, on crutches from spraining my ankle while dancing to "Wake Me Up Before You Go-Go" (a song I still can't listen to), two years into a rocky relationship that would putter along for another six. On the edge of graduating from college in Michigan, then moving to Virginia of all places, I didn't know at the time that I barely had any sense of self or that that was why I had such a hard time not only making friends, but finding any kind of community. I had always just chalked it up to being an introvert. Who needs to talk to people every day, right?

Cliché as it feels now, the first place I ever really felt like I could be myself was in the crowd at a Hold Steady show. I didn't know anybody (and didn't want to!) so there was no risk of embarrassment, no worries about taking up too much space, no pressure to make myself small or motionless, or not to dance. In retrospect, I can see that it was probably the first time that I could have a personality—it's funny to see that as the start of "becoming myself," when I was also in a relationship that was going to lead me all over most of the Midwest, mid-Atlantic, and Tennessee.

"You can make him like you," Craig said, and I was twenty-four and pumping my fist in celebration. Fuck yeah, I could make him like me. Sex is easy and guys were easier. Even introverts need to fuck.

That was the last time I got to see The Hold Steady before they went on hiatus, but as I was getting older, that truth stuck in my head. It stuck in my head when I heard that I was not a "good hang," a thing I now understand means "if you aren't having sex with the band, it's time to go home." It stuck in my head outside of romantic relationships when someone told me they didn't talk to me anymore because they had heard everything I have to say. It stuck in my head when I felt like I needed to work just a little harder for the cool girls at work to think I was . . . well . . . cool.

And it turns out that when you're applying and interviewing for jobs, the trick is that you just have to make them like you. I practiced and it worked. And when you're twenty-six and lovesick and certain, proximity seems like an attractive thing, so I moved to Nashville. When you want to get into a clique, emulate them a little harder—get the GAP sweater, drink Veuve Clicquot. Adapt.

Change. You can make him like you.

It stuck in my head when, after the band reformed and began playing shows again, I felt like I was there as someone else's accessory, which was a new feeling for me. I had always loved The Hold Steady independently (no, our boyfriends didn't bring us here), but for the first time, the Internet did what the Internet does and I knew people who would be in the crowd. I was still not convinced that I needed any friends—I'd moved through life that long without establishing any real connections—but I had enough practice on how to make them like me.

It's funny that it didn't take much work, though. It turns out that there are people who don't care if you're a good hang, who don't expect you to put out just because you're a woman in a male-dominated space, people who understand if you don't text back, people who send Veuve Clicquot to your house because your pandemic wedding got canceled and instead, you just signed papers in your living room.

Turns out that when you meet people who are also at their most honest in dark rooms covered in cheap beer, confetti, fresh margs, sweat, spilling wine in the pit, hobbling up to the front of the stage on crutches, it doesn't really take that much to make them like you.

—Desi Lynne Thorne

OVERHEARD AT A HOLD STEADY SHOW

Some background: I used to be a music journalist. In fact, I interviewed Craig and Tad in 2006 for the dearly departed *Tiny Mix Tapes,* thinking I was some kinda female Lester Bangs (or more realistically, the professor who assigned the story—Alex Chilton biographer Holly George-Warren. Hi, Holly). These days I'm a publicist (the real enemy), and everything I write is either way too long—or short, clipped, and neatly organized. I was never much good at moderation. You get the latter of the two options in this case. It's impossible for me to write objectively or coherently about anything this close to my heart. The best way for me to share it with you is presenting it at arm's length.

I was talking to my friend Mikey the other day about why I love movies from the '70s and early '80s so much (one exception being *Grosse Pointe Blank*). They're modern enough to be recognizable as vaguely representative of the way we live today, but there's a sheen—an amber-tinted overlay—that keeps the emotions from seeming similarly current. They're below the surface. I use movies like *Born to Win, The Anderson Tapes,* and *Klute* to feel things that I don't feel safe enough to experience on my own. In case it's not obvious, Hold Steady songs work like that too. But I digress. I've gone on too long here.

Names and identifiers have been redacted to protect the not-so-innocent. In the end, only the girls know the whole truth.

> *"There are a lot of pissed-off girlfriends at this show tonight."*
>
> —ANONYMOUS, IRVING PLAZA, NEW YORK, 2006

> *"Someone just bit Ed. No, like, BIT him. With teeth. On the shoulder. I don't even know, man."*
>
> —THREE DIFFERENT PEOPLE AT VARIOUS POINTS IN THE NIGHT, THE ELECTRIC BALLROOM, LONDON, 2019

> *"No offense but, like . . . why are you guys even here? This band is for dads . . ."*
>
> —A DAD, CONFUSED ON MORE LEVELS THAN HE COULD POSSIBLY KNOW, BROOKLYN BOWL, 2021

> *"Okay, so the bar usually closes now but we promised we'd buy them out of booze, so they're staying open as long as we want them to."*
>
> —A HOTEL BAR, PHILADELPHIA, 2008

> *"Why is Galen throwing dollar bills again?"*
>
> —EVERYONE OVER A SPAN OF THREE YEARS

"How do I feel? I dunno . . . sparkly . . ."

—ANONYMOUS, BOSTON, YEAR UNKNOWN

"I'm going to arrest ALL of you if you don't leave my club right now."

—A BOUNCER WHO WAS DEMONSTRABLY NOT A COP NOR A CLUB OWNER, SOMEWHERE IN NEW ENGLAND, 2011

"Have you seen this band before? I think Separation Sunday *is probably their quintessential album."*

—A MAN, TO ME, AT WHAT WAS PROBABLY MY EIGHTIETH SHOW

"Hey, you're not supposed to be here!"

—VARIOUS, TO VARIOUS, OVER MANY YEARS AND IN MANY LOCATIONS

"That's the third punisher of the night. I gotta get out of here."

—ANONYMOUS, PHILADELPHIA, 2009

-Heidi Vanderlee

IF YOU THINK THE HOLD STEADY ISN'T FOR WOMEN, YOU HAVEN'T BEEN PAYING ENOUGH ATTENTION

In a 2014 interview promoting their album *Teeth Dreams*, Craig talked explicitly about the intentionality with which he writes female characters. It is something he's sensitive to, he says, asking the interviewer: "Have you been to a Hold Steady show? How many women do you see in the audience?" *Huh,* I remember thinking when first reading this interview, *I guess he's right.* But I had never made the connections.

I spent my adolescence listening to emo and hardcore, begging my parents to let me go to shows. Those sweaty crowds were the first time I felt like myself—shouting lyrics back at bands, pressing our bodies up against each other, screaming until our throats were raw. I loved the community and catharsis of it, feeling anonymous and a part of something bigger all at once. My childhood was mostly defined by frequent moves and school changes, an absentee parent—the things I talk about in therapy that I won't get into now. Discovering that live music could make me feel like this was the first time I imagined that I could be a part of something in the moment it was happening. I loved the way my body vibrated from the music, how my ears ached for days after, the

shared sweat on my T-shirts, the physicality of it all. For the first time, I was a part of something bigger than myself—not just running from or reacting to the chaos happening around me.

As it happens, those feelings were fleeting, and toward the end of my adolescence, I started to realize that these shows weren't spaces where I was welcomed or represented. I started to hear jokes about being someone's girlfriend, and I started getting questioned about how well I knew the bands onstage. I was an awkward, fumbling seventeen, not really fitting in anywhere, and it became clear that these shows were no exception. And so I aimed to become a more passive fan of music. I stopped seeking out shows, and those I did attend I went to with crossed arms, standing in the back of rooms. I was a passionate, obsessive music fan, but now I did it from the comfort and safety of my dorm room. Shows weren't a safe space for me anymore. That is, until my first Hold Steady show.

I'm pretty sure you've heard this one before, but it bears repeating: there is nothing quite like a Hold Steady show. And it's more than the songs, the hand motions, the inside jokes we know by heart now ("business"). It's more than just wondering if the band will end the night with "Killer Parties," more than passing out confetti. The first time I saw The Hold Steady, in a small waterfront bar in upstate New York, it felt, for the first time in my life, that I was home. I was welcomed warmly, room was made for me in the front row, as we all sang and sweat together. Here, finally, was a place where no one cared how loud you sang, how much space you took up, what you looked like. I met people from Minneapolis, Vancouver, Toronto, California, who were all as thrilled as I was. I cried during the keyboard crescendo of "First Night," shouted with emphasis and agreement during "You Can Make Him Like You." When Craig yelled that this was how a resurrection really felt, I knew he was right.

I looked up the next show the band was playing as soon as that one was over. I started frequenting the message boards. I had arrived, it seemed, at a unified scene.

So you can imagine my surprise in the fifteen years that followed when I found out The Hold Steady wasn't for me. When I read the articles and picked up on both the overt and subtle references. Hold Steady culture, if you are to believe Google search results, is about dudes hanging out with other dudes, drinking beers and doing Dude Shit. A man in a flannel shirt, craft beer. *We left the kids at home with our wives tonight, baby! Hangovers be damned!* Hold Steady culture, if you are to believe Google search results, is about many things, but women aren't among them. It all felt a little too familiar.

Sure, the reports are somewhat true. I am consistently one of a very small percentage of women in the audience, especially in the front row. Yet at this point, I'm friends with almost all of them. We have a giant group chat, we take trips together, we're in each others' weddings. We are tongue-in-cheek fixtures at shows, the Ladies of the Front Row, and wear this name with pride. But to imply that the only thing binding us together is the novelty of our status at shows is disingenuous at best and offensive at worst. We are women, and we like The Hold Steady, but it's not like we're the only ones in the world.

This is one of the most perplexing parts of this narrative—I have rarely, if ever, felt unwelcome at a Hold Steady show. For every guy in his forties who tries to tell me about *Separation Sunday,* there are ten more people I've known for years who I'm thrilled to see. My husband, who I turned into a Hold Steady fan, is way more common at shows than any dude who wants to know if my boyfriend brought me. And ultimately, if you think that there's something inherently masculine about getting together to have a good time and sing about the human experience, that's kind of your internalized misogyny, isn't it?

Reflecting on my adolescence years later, I realize that part of what pushed me out of those scenes as a teen was the notion that I was purely ornamental or in these spaces on a man's whim, for a man's pleasure. That I had any of my own agency as a woman was not an idea found in the songs or the culture of those shows—but that's not the same for The Hold Steady. It's in the music, it's in the lyrics, it's in the inclusivity of the shows. If you think The Hold Steady isn't for women, you haven't been paying enough attention.

I am, you are, she is, they are, we are all.

-Kayleigh Wanzer

HOLD STEADY SUPERFAN JERSEY MIKE VAN JURA DIED ON NOVEMBER 18, 2012. THE FOLLOWING IS AN EXCERPT FROM AN ARTICLE PUBLISHED IN KEYSTONE EDGE IN FALL 2011:

Keystone Edge: *Is there a show you're most proud of at this stage?*

Jersey Mike Van Jura: *I tell people this all the time, but it kind of starts and ends with The Hold Steady. At the time we got The Hold Steady in 2007, I'd been booking ABC for a few years, but up until then, we'd really been doing mostly local bands and singer-songwriters, nothing national. I had gotten turned on to The Hold Steady eight to ten months prior to this. I just reached out to see if we could get them. It was at the same time that their third album,* Boys and Girls in America, *was breaking. So it was just the time that they were still playing for six to eight hundred bucks to one or two hundred people. But between the time we confirmed the show and when the show actually was, they just exploded. We actually did it as a free show—every year ABC does an anniversary fest, sort of a customer-appreciation thing. About six hundred people showed up—and two hundred didn't even get in. There was a line down Walnut Street to get in. It was just bananas. That was sort of a turning point for us. We had been just doing local bands, and we had lights down and sound down, and then we pulled this off. From there, we got the Felice Brothers, Southern Culture on the Skids, Cracker, and now we're doing MMW, the Carolina Chocolate*

Drops. I'm proud of every show—each one has its own challenges, but it was with that that we really turned a corner and realized, We can do this.

Life really is fantastic. Simultaneously fortunate and unfortunate. You need bad to recognize good. You need suffering to recognize happiness. A bit of a shame, but still wonderful. Did we know The Hold Steady existed? Yes. Did we know Mike had a lot of friends, was doing well, and people were aware of him? Yes. But did we know that there was a group of people who didn't just enjoy the same band and hanging out with each other but were unified well beyond that? No, not even close.

Sure, we were aware of THS, but my first time meeting Tad Kubler was in the basement of a funeral home. Traveling on three buses to quietly pay his respects—that's some commitment. There were several other people who showed up that and the next evening, and dozens, likely one hundred or more, who reached out to my parents and siblings in the days and weeks to follow. Having the *Stay Positive* infinity sign as an entry stamp at the Abbey bar makes a lot more sense in hindsight. As did finding out that a few dozen people had it tattooed on them as well. Mine would come later when things made more sense.

Each of us had our own experience, but none of us knew the extent of the love and support we'd have the privilege of receiving. Although Mike's children may not have experienced it directly, our family was better off because of THS, the Unified Scene, and many others. We were each the recipient of many good deeds and new friendships in the months and years that followed. Those early connections, especially when in a grief-fueled haze, mattered more than we realized. The impact of a Hedi, Howard, Kennedy, Rich, etc., etc., becomes a part of you forever. Nearly every day since, I give a moment of thought to pictures of Mike with Rich, Tad, and a poster from a (in) famous living room concert.

Mike was early. He was gathering emails, blogging, and doing a podcast before that was a thing. Seems like everyone wants to build a "community" today, but there is a purity to the community that developed fifteen or so years ago that most of today's will never get to. In the years since, it has been bittersweet, but more awesome, to see many of those people I met at the end of 2012 evolve and make their paths forward.

Going to a show in a random city, knowing there'll be people from the message boards and knowing there'll be someone in those shirts—that brings a certain amount of comfort. My early shows were a form of therapy, but the more recent ones I really get to see and feel them for what they are: a safety net of sorts that allows a band, or a friend of the scene, to know it will be a good night, but also provides a family a support system it didn't know it had.

-Billy Van Jura (brother of Jersey Mike Van Jura)

THE MESSAGE BOARD BECAME A PUBLIC SQUARE OF IDEA EXCHANGES

It was pink and black. Basic font. A message board. Primitive and mostly innocent by today's standards of Internet vitriol and "never read the comments" content. It was an online discussion site where people held threaded conversations in the form of posted messages. This is where the story of the Unified Scene begins.

Consider the time frame. The Hold Steady's first three albums were released without the connectivity of social media as we know it today. Facebook was five years away from existing in the public's consciousness and Instagram was another two years after that. *Almost Killed Me* (2004), *Separation Sunday* (2005), and *Boys and Girls in America* (2006) came out as MySpace began its rise and peak. Google began to overtake Yahoo! as the preferred Internet search engine. In the summer of 2007 the first iteration of the iPhone could be had for five hundred dollars and by the end of the year the number of texts sent exceeded the number of phone calls made. This was also the year that Twitter began its ascent in popularity.

Mike Van Jura loved Twitter. He joined in March of 2008 and in August of that year he "live tweeted" his entire road trip with Kennedy to see The Hold Steady—down to Norfolk, Virginia, and back up to the 9:30 Club in Washington, DC. Known on Twitter and the message board as "Jersey Mike," he was a local political rabble rouser and passionate music fan who unapologetically loved Huey Lewis and the News. At the small brewery bar he booked, he coerced bands like The Hold Steady, J. Roddy Walston and the Business, Frightened Rabbit, Cracker, Lucero, the Lumineers, and the Hackensaw Boys to a city, Harrisburg, Pennsylvania, which was on virtually no one's tour-routing maps. He had enthusiasm, he had energy. He was a force and he played an integral role in the Unified Scene.

The first version of The Hold Steady message board, forums.boysandgirlsinamerica.com, launched in the fall of 2006 just before the release of the namesake album. The message board was one of the few online sources where one could learn about the band in their early days. It was a place for fans to share their thoughts on the music and their experiences at the shows. It grew. It escalated. Fans joined in from all over the world—Toronto, London, Leeds, Manchester, the Netherlands, Australia, and in the beginning it still felt like the band was everybody's favorite little secret and they could not wait to share their discovery with other music enthusiasts. When was The Hold Steady going to be the biggest band in the world?

With everyone selecting their own user names when joining the message board, the handles ranged from the demure (*Joelle, Emily, Aimee, Katieee, John K*), to the self-referential (*Almighty LK, TKalltheTime, Phils_fan, Greenhat, Motorben, LilHan, Franny Glass*), to the lyric-inspired (*Hoodrat, 212 Margarita, Sunny D, Hard Corey, So Much Joy*).

The fans came from all walks of life: students, teachers, writers, art directors, nurses, dudes in the military, and even a Bible salesman . . . plus, yeah, maybe two or three too many lawyers.

The message board developed into a home for deep dives into the band's lyrics and sleuthing the journey of the characters within the songs. It was a depot for guitar chords and tablature for the musically inclined and a place to exchange mixtapes, errr, mixed *CDs,* for others. There were roll calls for shows while tickets and travel were occasionally stealthily provided for some prominently active Unified Scene members who did not have the funds to make the gigs otherwise. Confetti-smuggling strategies and pre-show meetups were hashed out. Tattoo photos were shared as were baking recipes. Did you want to know about the band's tour of Australia in real time? Legendary guitar tech Dustdudes posted a tour diary. And, of course, we were all reminded, Brendan Rules with discussions of juice boxes and how early is too early to queue in line for a show.

The message board became a public square of idea exchanges and people began to get to know one another. Friendships developed. Love affairs blossomed. Nightclub Dwight had hopes of meeting Whiskey Daisy for the first time in New York City at the 2007 Prospect Park show. Among a sweaty, frenzied crowd that stampeded over the big donors' expensive restricted seating area, the two never connected. Nightclub Dwight had a revelation. He posited that if the people from the message board had shirts, like team-style shirts, they'd be able to find each other easier. The idea was floated to the message board.

Around the same time, a thread circulated about what the folks from the message boards should be named as a group. A faction wanted "Steadheads" and somebody else wanted something longer like the Kinks's "The Village Green Preservation Society." JWD suggested "the Unified Scene." It wasn't put to a vote—once the moniker was tied into the idea of the team shirts, it was cemented.

The shirts, obviously, were a unified effort and they came about organically if not secretively, as a surprise. Campfirewood vectorized a stock image suggested by Seann to be the logo for the Unified Scene. Inspired by the song "Massive Nights," it could be interpreted as two people swing dancing just as easily as one reaching to pick the other up off the floor—either way, it captured the feel of a supportive, inclusive, unified scene. Seann then fronted the money for the first run of shirts, beginning a tradition of folks volunteering to pay for a batch of a couple dozen shirts to distribute free to fellow unified brethren. It quickly extended overseas with Howard initially taking on the role in the UK. The shirts were customized on the backs with numbers for those who signed up for them on the message board. Fittingly, Stephanie got number 1 as she had literally been there since the band's first show ever at Northsix in Brooklyn.

The shirts made their debut at a show in Birmingham, Alabama, in late 2007, but the most memorable impression was at a peculiar venue, the Czar Bar, in the heart of Ybor City in January 2008. The newly christened Unified Scene had traveled from Portland, Pittsburgh, Denver, Chicago, Milwaukee, Brooklyn, Philadelphia, Washington, DC, and Fort Lauderdale. As the band was about to launch into their first song, the as-yet-to-be-released classic "Stay Positive," Craig looked down at the first few rows of the packed crowd and asked, "Hey, what are you guys doing here?"

The shirts even made a national TV appearance after comedian Andy Kindler interviewed several Unified Scene members at a show in Baltimore for a segment that aired when the band appeared on the *Late Show with David Letterman* in July 2008.

By the end of that year, Jersey Mike, with significant help from Brendan, moved the "old pink and black boards" to a new host with a new design and a URL that lives on today. Over the next several years people came and went, people fell in and out of love (and back in love?) with the band and each other. There was some attrition occasioned by aging and family responsibilities (*"'Cause the kids at their shows, they'll have kids of their own"*). Even Jersey Mike was unusually tepid on the band during a perceived lackluster period in the years following the *Stay Positive* album, but in late 2012 he caught the band at the Ottobar in Baltimore. That night he kept to himself mostly—staying in the back and away from the fray. His final post on the Unified Scene message board was:

> *I follow and love this band like most people follow their favorite football team—I've been to dozens of shows, etc. And when I say this show happened in the last twenty minutes, I mean it HAPPENED in the last twenty minutes.*
>
> *That stage invasion? FUCK! I totally got choked up when it was happening. So. Much. Joy.*

Mike Van Jura died one month later of a heart attack, on November 18, 2012. He was thirty-six years old.

In February of 2014, The Hold Steady returned to Harrisburg, Pennsylvania, to the same small brewery bar Jersey Mike had booked for years, to remember and celebrate him. The band began the show the way they usually end a show—the slow build of "Killer Parties" with Craig describing how there was *SO. MUCH. JOY.* to play onstage, and as the band was about to kick in, he screamed, "We're The Hold Steady, you're the Unified Scene, and WE FUCKING LOVE YOU!"

The feeling is mutual. Forever.

-Rich Tarbell

THEIR SHOWS WERE THE CLOSEST I'D COME TO A RELIGIOUS EXPERIENCE

I expect that many of you reading this discovered The Hold Steady at a similar time as I did, with the release of *Boys and Girls in America*. The fusion of classic rock, masterful storytelling, and punk rock spirit was immediately irresistible, and it sounded like nothing else I was listening to. The blue gatefold LP is one of the most prized items in my thirty years of record collecting.

I'd go on to see the band live several times. They quickly cemented themselves as one of my all-time favorite live bands. Their shows were the closest I'd come to a religious experience. Hearing the crowd sing along in unison was almost spiritual to me—*"Our psalms are sing-along songs,"* indeed.

Then, in March 2014, at the tenderish age of thirty-five, I suffered a serious hemorrhagic stroke. I spent the next few months in a hospital, mostly lying in bed. Throughout my rehabilitation, I was frequently advised to "stay positive." My youngest brother, Andrew, is a fellow Hold Steady fan, and he'd play music to me as I lay in bed, including the then recently released sixth album, *Teeth Dreams*, but especially the earlier song "Stay Positive," which now had an additional, poignant meaning to me.

My rehabilitation was long and arduous, and it would be almost six months before I'd return home. I could no longer use my left limbs, and recovery became centered around learning how to adapt to life as a disabled wheelchair user. There were times I felt like I couldn't handle it anymore, and I faced bouts of depression and anxiety, but the refrain of *"You gotta stay positive!"* helped keep me focused on my recovery. So, rather than "almost killing me," The Hold Steady actually helped to keep me alive. And while I never walked again, I learned to adjust to my new life, and I kept my mind, and my passion for music.

Fittingly, the first show I went to after my stroke was The Hold Steady at the Manchester Academy 2 on October 19, 2014 (accompanied by Andrew, and my lifelong friend and best man Mark Tulloch). Finally going to a show after my stroke felt immensely important to me, but this turned out to be no ordinary Hold Steady show (if there is such a thing). Unbeknownst to me, Andrew had contacted the band to tell them about how important this gig was to me following my stroke, as well as the role the song "Stay Positive" played in my recovery. During the set, Craig dedicated the song to me, which was a class move, and meant so much. More was to come. Craig met us after the show to say hello. The Hold Steady and the Unified Scene really is a genuine community filled with so much joy. To meet the man responsible for a song that was now so important to me was mind-blowing!

-Paul Twist

CRAIG WAS RIGHT UP FRONT NEXT TO BRUCE

I have numerous favorite moments from being part of The Hold Steady's Unified Scene: yes, my first time seeing them perform at the Stone Pony; the "Two Shows, Two Boroughs" at the Bowery Ballroom and the Music Hall of Williamsburg; hearing *Heaven Is Whenever* performed for the first time at Positive Jam, and so many more.

But my favorite THS memory is one where they only played one song (though Craig sang two), and it was not a THS song.

It was April 5, 2007, at Carnegie Hall. The show was "The Music of Bruce Springsteen." An impressive lineup of over twenty performers was there to pay tribute to Springsteen and his music, including Pete Yorn, Steve Earle, Patti Smith, and Jessie Malin with Ronnie Spector. According to the program, Odetta was to close the show with "57 Channels (And Nothin' On)," but I knew a little secret: there was still one group to be heard from—The Hold Steady!

They were not listed in the program and most there did not know who they were. The crowd sat back as the boys, in line with the night's previous performances, started with a slow-moving rendition of "Atlantic City." But as Craig sang, *"Meet me tonight in Atlantic City,"* Bobby slammed the skins and the crowd rose to their feet for a rousing THS-style anthem. I could hear among many of the audience, "Who are these guys?" It was one of those times where I felt justified in my life choices (at least musically).

While this would have been enough to qualify as my favorite Hold Steady moment, there was more.

If the rousing THS performance was not enough of a closing act, one more performer came out: the Boss himself. With an acoustic guitar and harmonica, he spoke briefly about how all night he felt like a ghost hovering over his own funeral. He then played a slowed-down version of "The Promised Land," followed by a rare solo acoustic "Rosalita."

But Bruce did not finish the song. He said something like, "Well, it's getting late, unfortunately. And this song is really long. Man, I wrote a lot of lyrics back then." He went on to summarize the protagonist's story, finally asking all of the night's stars to come out and join him on the hallowed stage to sing with him. Pushed on by his bandmates, Craig was right up front next to Bruce to swap "Rosalita" lyrics with Badly Drawn Boy.

Now *that* is my favorite Hold Steady memory!

—Mike Gales

I WAS COMPLETELY DEVASTATED THAT CRAIG WOULD GET TO KNOW ME AS A TERRIBLY AWKWARD TEENAGE PHONE CONVERSATIONALIST

One year for Christmas, I unwrapped a piece of paper that would change my life. The gift was a phone call with Craig Finn. This is one of the more personal gifts I've ever received. I was touched thinking about how my mom had navigated the universe of Hold Steady fandom to purchase a call with my all-time favorite lyricist. At the same time, I was completely devastated

that Craig would get to know me as a terribly awkward teenage phone conversationalist. I tacked the piece of paper on the wall of my freshman college dorm room like some magic talisman.

In September 2014, I was at Boston Calling with my best friend from high school. Matt Berninger and the Dessners made her swoon, and the National was playing that Friday, followed by THS on Saturday. Sophie and I spent hours during the car ride up to Boston speculating about the lyrical genius of our favorite musicians. THS had gotten me through my first year of college. After reading Dante's *Inferno* and Augustine's *Confessions* in a freshman-year humanities class, I submitted a half-baked final paper to a professor with the recommendation to listen to *Separation Sunday* to enhance the reading experience.

We were waiting for the National to come on when Sophie turned to me and asked about *the* phone call. "You mean you haven't done it yet?" I must have looked at her with a kind of pained expression because her tone softened and she said, "Why don't you just see if you can meet Craig in person while you're here?" The thought of Craig sparing a moment to speak with me during the festival seemed completely ridiculous. "Give me your phone," she demanded, and sent an email to the address listed on the talismanic paper.

That was how I found myself on the Hold Steady tour bus the next day, staring at Craig hunched over a table littered with postcards and pieces of crumpled paper, the entire place emanating "Chillout Tent." Sophie accompanied me and would say later how fun it was to see me meet my hero. Scrambling for content, I told Craig that he should write an album based on Dante's *Inferno*, with each track a different circle of hell that a hero like Holly from *Separation Sunday* has to make it through, with someone like Craig, or Virgil, as her guide. I left our phone-call-turned-in-person-meeting with a book recommendation—*The Miracle Life of Edgar Mint*—and with a postcard telling me in scrawled handwriting to stay positive.

It was mercilessly hot later that day at the THS show. I was deliriously happy and in the second row, feeling born again after a great conversation. After playing "Your Little Hoodrat Friend," Craig paused and said, "I'd like to dedicate this next song to my new friend Molly Robinson." In a state of euphoric disbelief, I reflexively looked around the crowd for another Molly Robinson. Then Sophie was next to me screaming, pointing, "This is her! THIS IS MOLLY!" A seven-foot-tall hulking man in front of us hoisted me up onto his shoulders as the band began playing the next song: *"Southtown girls won't blow you away . . ."*

-Molly Robinson

PHOTO CREDITS

FRONT COVER: Lisa Brown
FRONT ENDSHEETS: Britton Mundyr
PAGE 1: Kelly Shee
PAGE 3: Kelly Shee
PAGE 4: Rich Tarbell
PAGES 6–7: Kelly Shee
PAGE 9: Moh Azima
PAGES 10: Kelly Shee
PAGE 13: Linda Kay Lund
PAGE 14: Rich Tarbell
PAGE 17: Tad Kubler
PAGE 19: Tad Kubler
PAGE 20: Judson Baker
PAGES 22–23: Lee Allen
PAGE 23: Rich Tarbell
PAGE 24: Camie Heller
PAGES 27: Rich Tarbell
PAGES 28–29: Lee Allen
PAGE 30: Lee Allen
PAGE 33: Sanjay Suchak
PAGES 34: Sanjay Suchak
PAGE 37: Lee Allen
PAGES 38–39: Camie Heller
PAGE 40: Sanjay Suchak
PAGE 42: Moh Azima
PAGES 46: Kelly Shee
PAGE 48: Tad Kubler
PAGE 49: Tad Kubler
PAGE 50: Kelly Shee
PAGE 51: Tad Kubler
PAGES 53: Kelly Shee
PAGE 54: Camie Heller
PAGE 56: Lee Allen
PAGE 59: Craig Finn
PAGE 61: Rich Tarbell
PAGE 64: Lee Allen
PAGE 67: Rich Tarbell
PAGE 68: Rich Tarbell
PAGE 71: Tad Kubler
PAGE 72: Tad Kubler
PAGES 74: Kelly Shee
PAGE 77: Rich Tarbell
PAGES 79: Kelly Shee
PAGE 81: Tad Kubler
PAGE 82: Rich Tarbell
PAGE 85: Rich Tarbell
PAGE 86: Sanjay Suchak
PAGE 88: Craig Finn
PAGE 91: Kelly Shee
PAGE 95: Lee Allen
PAGES 96: Lisa Brown
PAGE 98: Tad Kubler
PAGE 101: Lee Allen
PAGE 102: Lee Allen
PAGE 103: Lee Allen
PAGES 105: Kelly Shee
PAGE 106: Tad Kubler
PAGE 108: Moh Azima
PAGE 111: Rich Tarbell
PAGE 113: Rich Tarbell
PAGE 116: Rich Tarbell
PAGES 119: Kelly Shee
PAGE 120: Rich Tarbell
PAGE 123: Rich Tarbell
PAGE 124: Rich Tarbell
PAGE 126: Rich Tarbell
PAGE 127: Lisa Brown
PAGES 128: Lisa Brown
PAGE 131: Tad Kubler
PAGE 132: Rich Tarbell
PAGE 134: Camie Heller
PAGES 136–137: Kelly Shee
PAGE 137: Rich Tarbell
PAGE 139: Rich Tarbell
PAGE 141: Rich Tarbell
PAGE 145: Tad Kubler
PAGE 147: Lee Allen
PAGES 148–149: Brendan Hilliard
PAGE 148: Rich Tarbell
PAGE 150: Rich Tarbell
PAGE 154: Lee Allen
PAGE 157: Rich Tarbell
PAGE 158: Tad Kubler
PAGES 161: Tad Kubler
PAGE 163: Kelly Shee
PAGE 164: Lee Allen
PAGE 166: Tad Kubler
PAGE 169: Rich Tarbell
PAGE 171: Tad Kubler
PAGE 172: Brendan Hilliard
PAGE 174: Rich Tarbell
PAGE 177: Tad Kubler
PAGE 178: Rich Tarbell
PAGE 180: Rich Tarbell
PAGE 182: Courtesy of Tad Kubler
PAGE 185: Tad Kubler
PAGE 187: Courtesy of Tad Kubler
PAGE 188: Rich Tarbell
PAGE 191: Rich Tarbell
PAGE 192: Lisa Brown
PAGE 195: Rich Tarbell
PAGE 196: Sanjay Suchak
PAGE 199: Rich Tarbell
PAGE 200: Lee Allen
PAGE 203: Tad Kubler
PAGE 204: Rich Tarbell
PAGE 206–207: Lisa Brown
BACK ENDSHEETS: Camie Heller
BACK COVER: Lee Allen

DUST PRIDE

POCO

CONSTRUCTIVE

MULTITUDE

THE SWISH

MAGAZINES

SEQUESTERED

PARTY PIT

MASSIVE NIGHTS

EARL

EXPLODE

STEVIE NIX

BARFRUIT

YEAH SAPPHIRE

ADDERALL

SWEET PAYNE

DJ'S

WMD

DISCOURAGED

HOODRAT

STAY POSITIVE

SLAPPED ACTRESS

~~mmmmmmmmm~~

RO

STATIONS

CHIPS AHOY!

ER PARK - PIER 26

CONSTRUCTIVE

~~HOT~~ SOFT LIGHT

HURRICANE J

WAIT A WHILE

THE SWISH

ROCK PROBLEMS

RAINBOW

CHIPS AHOY!

YOU CAN...

HOODRAT

CATTLE

STATIONS

SEQUESTERED

SOUTHTOWN

STAY POSITIVE

P